AN ACTION PLAN FOR TEENS

RECREATE YOUR WORLD

FIND YOUR VOICE, SHAPE THE CULTURE, CHANGE THE WORLD

RON LUCE

WITH CHARITY LUCE

Regal

From Gospel Light
Ventura, California, U.S.A.

Published by Regal
From Gospel Light
Ventura, California, U.S.A.
www.regalbooks.com
Printed in the U.S.A.

Library of Congress Cataloging-in-Publication Data
Luce, Ron.
Recreate your world : find your voice, shape the culture, change the world / Ron Luce ;
with Charity Luce.
p. cm.
Includes bibliographical references.
ISBN 978-0-8307-4639-2 (trade paper)
1. Christian teenagers—Religious life. 2. Christianity and culture—Christianity.
I. Luce, Charity. II. Title.
BV4531.3.L833 2008
248.8'3—dc22
2008026895

Rights for publishing this book outside the U.S.A. or in non-English languages are administered
by Gospel Light Worldwide, an international not-for-profit ministry. For additional information,
please visit www.glww.org, email info@glww.org, or write to Gospel Light Worldwide, 1957
Eastman Avenue, Ventura, CA 93003, U.S.A.

CONTENTS

INTRODUCTION

What you have in your hands will set you on a completely different path for the rest of your life. If you dare page through this book and grab a hold of what you are about to read, you are in for the incredible ride of your life.

At 16, when I first got turned onto Jesus, I realized that He changed my life so dramatically that everyone ought to have the chance to have the same change. I began to tell my friends at school and everyone I knew; I couldn't help it. That same passion drove my wife, Katie, and me to start Teen Mania 22 years ago, and it still drives us today as we lead Teen Mania, Acquire the Fire and BattleCry. What we do is all about a dream to change the world and let the love of Jesus reign in our lives—and in as many other lives as we can possibly influence.

You are about to discover the final ingredients you need to become part of this revolution. A revolution of love is not just an organization. It means people just like you, saying, "Jesus is real to me and I want to make Him real to the world." Dive in. Devour this, take notes, write down your ideas all the way through. Use this as it was designed to be used—as a launching pad to make you a freak of nature for God for the rest of your life. At the end of your life you want to look back and say, "Wow, my life *mattered*. I didn't just have a career, a family, and some hobbies. My life mattered to the kingdom of God. It mattered to the direction of this nation and to the young people in the generation after me."

It starts now while you are young. It takes a God-breathed determination in your heart that drives you to say, "I refuse to go through my teen years without making a difference."

SECTION I

WHY RECREATE?

CHAPTER 1

GENERATION OUT OF CONTROL

A sly web has been spun. A conveyer belt has been constructed. The bait has been laid and the prey has been clearly and artfully selected. The stability of our generation is at stake. This is a tragic phenomenon that we are about to describe. We'll illustrate it with a story you are likely to find familiar.

The Britney Factor

I suppose the only people who don't know who Britney Spears is would have to have lived in a cave for the past 10 years. The stories of her recent public meltdowns have hit every tabloid and news show in the land. Her life seems to be spiraling out of control, with one bad decision after another broadcast for the world to see, resulting in unbearable public humiliation.

She was a teenager when she got her "big break." With an air of innocence and charm she sang and danced for the masses as her first album took flight. It certainly appeared to be a "big break" for her. In reality, it was not just her big break, but the recording industry's break, as they are constantly on the lookout for new talent to exploit (I mean, promote). *She was perfect for their use.* Like a fresh "product" hot off the market, she was sold to the teens and preteens who eagerly wait for the next CD or icon to emerge.

The story behind Britney was that as long as they could keep her in front of people, it wouldn't just make her money but all of the corporations and producers would also keep raking in the cash. These executives need new "eye-candy" to appeal to new audiences; so much of their business is to answer the question, *Who can we discover and make big so that we can sell more stuff?* She might make a dollar per CD, but they're making five or more per CD. She might make extra for an appearance on MTV, but its promotional value only sells more of her music. MTV makes hundreds of millions of dollars off of people like her. As a result, they will do whatever they have to do to keep pop icons like Britney visible to keep young viewers' eyeballs on the screen. The more teens that watch, the more they make from advertising.

Without much say from her parents, innocent Britney began to sing about the fact that she's "not that innocent." Her music videos got raunchier, her lyrics got dirtier, and her clothes started falling off like apples on trees. Her new identity started flashing the rampage of her videos and magazine appearances. Then there was the unforeseen lip-lock with Madonna on national TV during the MTV awards in 2003.[1] It seems the more she pushed toward the edge, the further she needed to go to keep the next wave of paparazzi satisfied.

Her visibility continued to mesmerize crowds; all the while the industry (that is MTV, Viacom, record companies, clothes and makeup companies) was making more off her persona. They maintained a very vested interest in keeping her public and giving her hints that would keep her in the public eye.

Finally, in September 2007, she was a last-minute addition to the MTV awards show to debut her new album. She was originally supposed to appear with magician Chris Angel, but he pulled out when he realized this was not going to be good. On the occasions when she actually came to rehearsals, with martini in hand, she found it hard to practice her dance routine. It was blatantly obvious to everyone that she was not ready for a live TV appearance. Both her wardrobe and her music needed some serious work. Yet MTV refused to pull her appearance, although it was evident that public humiliation awaited her.[2] They knew that killer ratings were in store for them, and that's all they cared about.

While millions of people have been entertained and seduced by Britney, the industry has made millions of dollars. And while millions of people have been appalled and enthralled by her humiliation, the industry has made millions of dollars more. This cycle is part of a *machine* that uses people for the sake of ratings, not caring what it does to them in the process. Britney is not the only one. Many other young stars are in the *machine*. Think about Lindsay Lohan, the Olsen twins and Macaulay Culkin.

There are other casualties of this culture machine. Fans of the stars occupy the other end of the spectrum; the machine needs stars, but they also need fans to buy the albums and go to the concerts. The industry's job is to sell, sell, sell. It doesn't care what it sells or to whom it sells, just as long as the money comes in. The antics of humiliated, confused and unpredictable Britney Spears are a picture of what the pop culture machine is doing to many teens trapped in the vortex of its destructive agenda.

Amy Winehouse is a prime example of what the machine does to people. In 2008 her album *Back to Black,* featuring the hit song "Rehab," won five Grammy awards. Amy was unable to receive the award in person because she had been denied a visa to enter the United States due to her recent drug troubles.[3]

Think of the message this is sending out. Winehouse, who was once reportedly seen wandering around in her nightgown strung out on

drugs, and who was recently accused of assaulting someone, is the person the machine chooses to exalt, giving millions of young girls the opportunity to emulate her.

The pop culture machine "cares" for you the same way it cares for Britney. The machine devours them and then spits them out. Lives are destroyed within the machine, as well as influenced by the product of the machine. Then the machine rinses and repeats, looking for the next product to sell and the next person who will buy it.

How the Machine Works

There are about 71 million young people who make up what is currently the largest generation in American history, 33 million of whom are actually teenagers right now.[4] Their number is so great that most marketers perceive them as an untapped gold mine—if they can just "embezzle" their attention and then sell to them. Right now, teens spend about $150 billion a year[5] and influence about another $200 billion of their parents' spending.[6] This is huge, but nothing compared to the lifetime spending potential of these young consumers. Marketers have documented that 13 is the age that many decisions are made for life-long buying habits. It's called the branding age (just like cattle, they wear a brand—they identify with a product so much that they buy it and are proud of it). So if the machine can get them to like a drink, a clothing line or a musician by the time they are 13, they will probably buy those brands for the rest of their life.

"Of course, it is not the marketing that is the problem," as I told Vicki Mabrey from ABC News *Nightline*. "People are going to sell stuff and others will buy. It is the marketing without a conscience, without caring what you sell to teens and how it shapes them that is the problem." Much of what is sold to teens (and to children) is media driven (whether it's video games, websites, music, TV or movies). When confronted, most makers of media are quick to excuse their culpability by pointing to the parents who are responsible for what their kids see. While this is indeed true (we will deal with it at greater length in a later chapter), their entire machine is unmistakably aimed at selling to kids. If they could *not* sell to them, they would be out of business. They would not even risk creating the product unless they were convinced they could capture a massive group of people who would buy their stuff. The media actually thrives on the fact that most parents are either irresponsible or have no idea what they are selling to their kids.

Some parts of this culture machine (that actually manufactures teen culture) are staggeringly massive. Take Viacom for example; they own Nickelodeon, Nick Jr., MTV, MTV2, VH1, Comedy Central, BET, Logo (the gay channel), as well as other media outlets. They have what they call a "cradle to grave" strategy. They start when kids are very young, get-

ting them enamored with pop icons as they are baby-sat by Nickelodeon. Soon, they graduate to Nick Jr. and MTV, and their appetite for music and their desire to emulate the clothes, the vogue, and every gesture of the hottest star is kicked into full function mode. They are happy to keep people occupied through every era and epoch of their life, making money as they maneuver them through their entire life cycle.

PBS reported, in their special "Merchants of Cool" a few years ago, how MTV has developed a prototype of what they want the teens watching their network to become.[7] *Mooks* are what they call the boys. They found that the more crass humor they built into their programming, the more teenage boys would watch. So they intentionally built new programs like *Jackass,* and hosts such as Tom Green, that constantly parade the Mook lifestyle (irresponsible, perverted, apathetic, use of crude humor, disrespectful) into new programs and MTV movies. The more they can get teens to watch, the more teens will want to be like what they see. And the more they try to become everything the media offers, the more they sit on their couch and are consumed by the very thing they're becoming; all the while Viacom is making lots of money. They are producing a whole generation of Mooks who are glued to their couch and consuming massive doses of the media that is created to keep them on the couch.

Midriffs are what they label the girls. The message they're sending is, "Hey, if you've got it, flaunt it, even though you are underage. Act like you're older than you really are." So they promote stars like Christina Aguilera, the Pussy Cat Dolls, and, of course, Britney, to be the poster children of all this. They show spring break programs of high school and college girls showing skin and getting drunk. Of course, they never expose the stories of girls who get raped, get a disease or end up pregnant. Girls then stay glued to their favorite starlet and, of course, mimic her clothing and lifestyle—except that girls (unlike those on TV) are having to pay the consequences of the lifestyle, like getting pregnant or catching diseases.

Viacom boldly proclaims, "We don't advertise to this generation; we own this generation." And in many ways it does, all while making about

$3.27 BILLION in profit from destroying our generation of young people in the U.S. and around the world.[8]

Is it any wonder that 16-year-old Jamie Lynn Spears (Britney's younger sister), star of Nickelodeon's *Zoey 101,* turned up pregnant? The machine has done to her what it has been doing to millions of other girls from all over the world. It's no surprise that *Nick Jr.* did not cancel the show. Then they would have to admit that what Jamie Lynn has done is a shameful thing. Thus, millions of preteens now have this 16-year-old icon looming before them as a role model.

This machine is hungry. It must be fed. It needs more stars to control and exploit (what they would call *giving them a* "big break"). Who is really getting the big break? They also need fans to vend to. In either case, they do not care about the ultimate effect their machine has on its victims. Who's next? Is it the sweet Miley Cyrus of *Hannah Montana* fame, who will be sexualized to keep interest piqued? Will you be the next Mooks and Midriffs to be produced by this machine?

Take a look at these headlines of news stories in the past year:

- 12-Year-Old Beats Toddler to Death with Bat, Police Say[9]
- Teacher Arrested After Offering Good Grades for Oral Sex[10]
- Birth Leave Sought for Girls[11]
- Colorado Teens Accused of Killing 7-Year-Old Girl with "Mortal Kombat" Game Moves[12]

THE CULTURE MACHINE IS HUNGRY. IT MUST BE FED. IT NEEDS MORE STARS TO CONTROL AND EXPLOIT.

- Teen Accused of Trying to Rape 62-Year-Old Woman[13]
- 6th-Grade Teacher Gets 10 Years in Prison for Sex with 13-Year-Old Boy[14]
- Michigan Teen Shooter Stopped Taking Medication Before Killing[15]
- Nevada Suspect Arraigned in Case of Videotaped Rape of Girl, 3[16]
- U.S. Prosecutor Accused of Seeking Sex with Girl, 5[17]
- Texas Girl, 6, Found Hanging in Garage Was Sexually Abused[18]
- Michigan Mom Gets 12 to 22 Years for Sex "Contract" on Underage Daughter[19]
- Man Gets 20 Years for Bizarre Internet Love Triangle Murder[20]
- Four College Students Shot Execution-Style in Newark, N.J.[21]
- Young Mother Charged After Her 10-Month-Old Boy Recorded Sipping Gin and Juice[22]

Look at the crop of fruit generated from this culture-marketing machine. See what it has done and is doing to your peers. Now you can see why we must all pull together to re-create your generation.

All those who dare to venture forward in an exciting journey of shaping the culture—both for our family and for our whole generation—continue reading and prepare for the most stirring adventure of your life, because dreamers are the ones who spark revolution.

CHAPTER 2

WHOSE DREAMS ARE SHAPING YOU?

As we've been talking about the culture machine, you may find yourself wondering:

Who runs this machine?

Who invented the machine?

And who keeps it going?

Because whoever is running the machine is shaping our culture and whoever shapes culture ends up shaping most of the people in our culture.

Once, when Jesus was talking to a crowd about His eccentric cousin, John the Baptist, Jesus decided to set the record straight. John was kind of a mystery to people; they didn't know what to expect from him because they'd heard some pretty wild things about him. What kind of a guy lives on locusts and sports animal skins? But during Jesus' conversation with these people, John was in prison for speaking the truth about God. And Jesus asks, "What did you go out into the desert to see? A reed swayed by the wind?" (Luke 7:24-25, *NIV*). John would not scatter in the face of danger, and Jesus wanted people to know what a true follower looks like. He was saying, *When you look at John, you don't see a guy who's blown back and forth like a reed in the wind; you see a guy who knows who he is and what he stands for.* Think about reeds. They're a bunch of thin blades of wheat, and when the four winds blow, the reeds are tossed about in every direction.

In the same way the reed gets blown in the wind, the culture tries to blow us back and forth, shaking us from our foundation, trying to twist what we believe and shape how we live. Who are these people who are trying to "blow us in the wind"? Predominately the people who are shaping culture are the people who speak loudest. And how do they speak loud? They speak through movies, music, television, styles and advertising. Our ferocious appetite for culture keeps us wanting these things—these new pants, TV shows, albums coming out, and stuff on the Internet. Are these just TV programs, movies and pants, or is there somebody who actually designs these things to feed to us? Are they desires that we spontaneously come up with or are we cleverly lured into the traps because of the ads we see and the shows we watch that create a want for these things inside of us?

Think about it for a moment. These creative executives who create the products and end up creating our culture start somewhere with a dream. Every movie that was ever made started with a conversation. Someone was having coffee with someone else and said, "Wouldn't it be a great idea to make this movie and make this point? It would be very exciting." They scribbled it down on a napkin somewhere and then went and got a writer and a director and a producer; they went and got a film company; they found sponsors and finances and ultimately made the movie that we pay money to go see. *It started with someone's dream.* They either really had a dream about making a story into a film, or they really had a dream about making money and thought of a story that would help them make that money. Either way, it is still *their* dream that ends up shaping you.

Sometimes they use their dream purposely to try to influence either with violence or sex or some idea they want to communicate in the film. Sometimes their motivation is purely money and they don't care how it will affect you if you're watching. For example, there are *over a thousand* studies that now show that the more violence you watch in TV or movies, the more likely you are to be violent. Whether that's shooting or beating people up, whatever. Even though there are new studies that prove this coming out every year, the hostility and aggression in our society shown in media is getting even worse. You see, they don't really care about you; they care about making money and they fall back on, "Well, it's the individual's choice and responsibility. We can't be held responsible for what they do."

The same goes for advertising. There are so many ads for products that are sexual in nature. The product has nothing to do with sex or even a guy, or girl, or a relationship. It's just that if they can slap a bikini on a girl, she might be more likely to help them sell hamburgers—as in the case of the Carl's Jr. commercial featuring Paris Hilton.

Think about music, for example, and how much teenagers listen to music. Teens listen to as much as 30 hours of recorded music alone—not to mention radio. But these executives who own and run the music companies that produce violent or perverted records don't care what their music might do to you, and neither do many of the band members as long as they can sell their stuff. They might be angry and depressed and so they write their songs about that. So you might listen to their songs five million times and they wonder why you're angry and depressed—maybe even suicidal or just hating life. These band members and executives don't love you; they don't care about you. How can a person love someone and mess up their lives at the same time? All they care about is themselves and making a name. Their dream for making money has resulted in so many of you, or people just like you, feeling depressed and lonely and maybe even wanting to end their lives.

What about the guys who make the video games? These are the guys that essentially have created a blood-splattering extravaganza in the name of entertainment. It's designed for you to spend hours and hours of your life on the very same technology used in the military to teach soldiers to shoot guns in wars; yet, they say for some reason that "it won't hurt you." So we have stories of teenagers in jail now because they planned and carried out a murder, but they planned it with the same tools they used in the video game. Once again, they don't care about you. Someone had a dream to make some money; they just wanted to sell a million copies of a video game. But they don't care about how it's shaping your generation—how it's turning your peers into hurting, broken and violent people.

What about the makers and manufacturers of teen clothing lines? These guys at Abercrombie and Fitch, Hollister or Hot Topic don't care what might happen to you if you're a young lady and you're 14 years old and they're showing you how great it is to show all kinds of skin. They don't care if it might draw an older guy to look at you and try to woo you to do things that you would normally only want to do after you are married. Once again, their dream to make money, to make a name for themselves, to sell a lot of their product, ends up in you paying a price.

And of course, there's the more massive perversion of Internet pornography. The people who are creating the cutting edge technology they use for Internet porn do not care about you. All they care about is selling their product. They don't care if they are exploiting you, getting you to watch it or act in it or make you want to mimic it in pictures on MySpace. All they care about is that they're making their money and it doesn't really matter what it might do to you.

The point you might find in all of these examples is that much of what is shaping your generation *you did not invent*, and none of your peers invented—it was invented for you—someone did it to you. You have been tricked and deceived, and they're profiting at your expense. Their dreams are shaping you and, in many cases, creating a culture of destruction for your generation. So, every time you pick up this book, you're gaining the ability to see through their lies. And on each page, you will discover the secrets to shaping your culture. By the end you'll have what it takes to reach down into the deepest part of *yourself* and dream dreams that will shape your generation and blow you away.

Did you feel that? I think I just felt the foreshock of an earthquake.

YOU HAVE BEEN TRICKED AND DECEIVED, AND OTHERS ARE PROFITING AT YOUR EXPENSE. THEIR DREAMS ARE SHAPING YOU AND, IN MANY CASES, CREATING A CULTURE OF DESTRUCTION FOR YOUR GENERATION.

CHAPTER 3

THE INSIDIOUS GRIP OF CULTURE

Most of what influences us in culture is not obvious. It's sly, it's sneaky, it's deceptive, it's addictive, and it's attractive. It lures us into a bit of a trap by creating a desire inside of us that makes us want to go back to it like a dog returning to it's vomit. It's insidious.

The Latin word for "insidious" is translated "to lie in wait for."[1] If we look carefully, we will begin to catch traces of an insidious plan in our culture that is designed to entrap and beguile. This plan is devised by an insidious enemy, whose nature is treacherous and deceitful. The plan is carried out in an inconspicuous manner, seemingly harmless, but actually having a significantly grave effect, like an undetected disease.

Lions have to be close to their prey before they begin their attack. They often kill their prey near some form of cover or at night. They sneak up near their victim until they are about 98 feet away. Typically, several female lions work together and encircle the herd from different points. Once they have closed with a herd, they usually target the prey

that is closest to them. Their attack is short and powerful—they attempt to catch the victim with a fast rush and final leap. The lions usually kill their prey by strangulation.[2]

This plan lures us into its trap by taking us to higher levels of entertainment and adventure than we've ever known. Then it wraps its jaws around our necks and chokes the life out of us. Too often, even "good Christian" homes have found that they have been invaded by an amoral culture of destruction. But too many have found out too late, after living through a nightmare of a family life that proved to be a living hell.

Our culture is rife with stories of young people who have become destructive with their lives, even those who were raised in "decent" families. This behavior is sometimes only hurtful to the person feeling the pain; and other times, the behavior becomes life-threatening to others. Recently, some of the most horrifying crimes have been committed by teenagers. Often the violence is even more shocking when we think about the wholesome families that these kids were raised in. Somehow they didn't grasp the values of their parents; they just missed it. Somehow, whether or not parents have tried to pass on the family values, it just hasn't stuck.

Just rewind about 50 years and you'll find that most movies and television shows were squeaky clean. The episode of the hit show *I Love Lucy* shocked audiences in the scene in which Lucille Ball and Desi Arnaz were seen in the same bedroom—oh yeah, they also had two separate beds AND they were married. People were appalled that TV would expose such a private situation. Times have changed, people. It's pretty obvious that the values that belong to one generation are simply not being handed down to the next. Let's look at a few snapshots of what is happening in our culture today.

Matthew Murray

On December 9, 2007, we watched in amazement the reports of yet another shooter attacking a church, injuring and even killing some of the members. This was only hours after the same shooter killed two staff at the local Youth With A Mission (YWAM) campus. The shooter, Matthew

Murray, was raised in a Christian home. Both of his parents were active members of their church and avid followers of well-known Christian preachers. They nurtured both of their boys in a Christian home-school program until they were old enough to pursue their own path of life. One son chose to go to a Christian university, while Matthew chose to attend YWAM and then worked on staff with a YWAM youth program. On the outside, Matthew and his family seemed to have everything going for them. But Matthew's inner life was inhabited by turmoil and despair.

Because Matthew is no longer alive, no one can really know what was going on inside of him, but his journal postings indicate that he was indeed searching for truth in a murky pool of teachings—messages as diverse as those from the Christian church to lyrics by the "shock rock" musician Marilyn Manson to writings of the late British occultist Aleister Crowley. However, even before Matthew began listening to Marilyn Manson, there is some evidence that he was depressed and even suicidal at the age of 17. What happened? How does a young boy raised in a Christian home not only become suicidal, but eventually homicidal?[3]

Eric Harris and Dylan Klebold

In recent years, there have been many shootings in America, but none that have shocked or shaken the world like the 1999 massacre at Columbine High School, near Denver, Colorado. After murdering 12 students and a teacher, and wounding 23 others, Eric Harris and Dylan Klebold committed suicide and sealed the vault of their journey on this horrific day in history. However, upon examination of both boys' families, there is nothing out of the ordinary that would raise suspicion of a violent behavior in these children. Eric's dad was enlisted in the Air force, which required relocation, as any military family would have experienced. After he retired, they moved to Littleton, Colorado, where he worked for a company that makes military flight simulators. His wife worked for a local caterer. Eric's parents tried to impress their strong work ethic onto their kids and were always supportive of their sporting activities. His friends knew them as "good parents." It wasn't until Eric was in high school that his parents started to see any reason to be concerned about his behavior, which prompted them to take him to a psychiatrist.

A "picture-perfect" family is how their neighbors described Dylan's family. Both parents graduated from Ohio State University. His dad was a real-estate agent and his mom was an employment counselor. The family attended a Lutheran church, and the two Klebold brothers completed their confirmation classes in accordance with Lutheran tradition. They also observed many Jewish rituals at home because Dylan's mom had a strong Jewish heritage. Unfortunately, even with strong religious influence and supportive parents, Dylan still ended his life immersed in a world of violence and hatred.[4]

Jamie Lynn Spears

When she was only six weeks old, Jamie Lynn Spears began following big sister Britney around the entertainment world as Britney performed for an off-Broadway show entitled *Ruthless*. At the age of 10, Jamie Lynn continued in her sister's footsteps by appearing in a Clorox commercial, which spiraled into a whirlwind of television appearances and regular roles on sitcoms. Even before Jamie Lynn was born, her parents were always hardworking and supportive. They paid for Britney's singing, dancing and gymnastic lessons no matter how financially challenging it may have been.

Jamie Lynn's father was a building contractor, her mother, a first-grade teacher, and they worked hard to keep their kids in private school along with their extracurricular activities. They gave Jamie Lynn the same amount of support that Britney had, which is what helped propel her into a prominent role on the TV sitcom *Zoey 101*. However, at 16, Jamie Lynn's career was cut short with the news of her pregnancy in December 2007. The father is a 19-year-old boy she met at church and had moved in with for a while before the pregnancy was announced. Although Jamie Lynn is a celebrity, her story is no different from those of many other teenage girls across the country—many who also come from *good* families.[5]

OUR CULTURE <u>DOES</u> SNEAK UP, GRAB, AND DESTROY LIVES. WE'VE GOT TO BE THE ONES WHO OUTSMART THE CULTURE AND PROTECT OUR GENERATION FROM BEING WRECKED AND DESTROYED.

Ben Thompson

Pastors' kids sometimes get into more trouble than all the kids in the church combined. Ben Thompson definitely proved to be one of those kids. Even though his parents had been pastors for 30 years, Ben still managed to find himself in the middle of a gang war with the Crips, one of the most notorious gangs in North America. He became involved in drive-by shootings and was shot at on more than one occasion. Even though he escaped the gangster life, Ben continued to be involved in destructive activity. After opening his own line of clothing, he began promoting it at nightclubs in Southern California, where he got caught up in alcohol and drug abuse as well as sexual activity. He became addicted to Speed, was suicidal, and then got a girl pregnant who eventually had a miscarriage. Although he turned to his parents and to God for help after hitting rock bottom, the question still remains: How did he get there in the first place?[6] Looks like the world did more training of this teen than his father, who is a pastor.

Culture Affects Us

One thing all of these tragic stories have in common is that the kids were raised in "good, church-going" families. Whether it was their peers or a fierce grasp of the media on their hearts, each of them was somehow manipulated and seduced by influences around them. These influences shaped their values more than their parents shaped their values.

Probably everyone reading at this moment can easily call to memory faces of kids who used to be in your church who found themselves in some serious trouble, possibly turning up pregnant or ending in some kind of tragedy that happened in your town. The point here is that we don't instantly see how the culture affects us. This is because we've consumed years and years and thousands of hours of influence from the very coolest, trendiest approaches of communication. But it *does* sneak up, grab, and destroy lives. We've got to be the ones who outsmart the culture and protect our generation from being wrecked and destroyed by this insidious culture.

CHAPTER 4

DREAM KILLERS

I know what you are thinking: "That kind of thing would *never* happen to me. I could never be the guy who grew up in church and ended up doing horrible things." Well that is probably what they thought. Maybe it won't influence you to do something tragic like that, but it might change you in ways you cannot imagine.

There is another kind of tragedy that happens all the time. It's a lot more subtle and it affects many more people. These elements of culture that are so addicting decapitate any dream that you might have to make a difference in the world. We will call them dream killers. Think about how it works.

Media

Think about media. How many movies do you watch in a week? How many in a month? How many hours of TV do you watch per week? Statistics show the average teenager is in front of the screen between 35 and 55 hours a week between a computer and TV screen. Think of all the media that is being absorbed. Think of all the dreams other people have created. Think of all the time you have spent watching other people's dreams. Even if it wasn't negative media, just mediocre media, at the very least it is stealing from you the hours of life that you spend watching their stuff. It is stealing from your ability to dream and make a difference in the world. Instead of being a dreamer and changing the world, you are watching someone else's dream and being entertained by it.

I'm not saying that you can never watch another movie or TV show. We've just got to be careful. While we are being entertained and paying them to entertain us, it is stealing from us the energy and time to go make a difference ourselves. Let's think of some of the other phenomena that kill our dreams.

Music

Let's talk about music for a moment. Teenagers spend hours and hours every day listening to music. In the name of multi-tasking, you may say, "I can listen to music and do whatever." Whether we realize it or not, the ideas that artists are writing about and singing about shape us as we listen. Just like a friend who you invite over and then who decides to rearrange all your furniture, the music enters our mind and changes how we think.

Part of who you are is the way you think and the ideas you have. Often our dreams become drowned out by a flood of constant noise. Not to say that music can never inspire us; but if we substitute our own creativity for the ideas of others, something is lost. You have something inside you that *no one else* on this planet can offer but you.

How you see the world and what you do about it is called *your creativity*. Creativity isn't just something for the "artsy" people. Each person thinks and feels and dreams differently.

If you are a lover of music, instead of just drinking it all in, maybe it is time for your melodies and lyrics to inspire others. At the very least, others' musical ideas are occupying the time you could be spending dreaming your own dream and writing your own music.

Dumbed-down Reading

Think of all the music magazines, teen pop-idol magazines, and comic books out there. Millions of teenagers follow this stuff as if the most important thing in their life is to know what's going on with everyone who lives inside a television or silver screen. They just can't wait to find out who is dating whom, and who was seen with whom. It seems like the most essential thing. We have a culture chock-full of pop icons. Instead of living our life, we watch them live their life and we are entranced by it. If you had five bucks for every hour you've invested in following the lives of celebrities, how rich would you be? Instead of living our own dreams, we often watch someone else live theirs or, in some cases, watch their lives come crashing down.

The Internet

Hasn't enough already been said about MySpace and Facebook? Think about all the other ways teens spend their time on things like Second Life. There is a direct correlation between the amount of time spent on the Web and people who feel depressed. Instead of getting what we really want—authentic relationships with people who we connect and share our heart with—we are feeling more and more isolated. We say we have "more friends" than ever before because we have accepted them as a friend on MySpace. (But then we get mad at them and just block them.) Is that what happens in a real friendship? In real life, don't you have to look at that person in the eye and work things out—sometimes even ask for forgiveness?

The point here is, again, that we spend our time talking to counterfeit friends. Have you ever gone in to check your MySpace account and ended up, four hours and several bags of chips later, connecting to other people's sites but missing the close friendships you're really looking for?

As a young person reading this, it's important for you to realize that God has a big dream for your life. With culture hammering us and trying to steal our attention and our time, they serve as killers and murderers of any kind of dream that you might have. I encourage you now to think about the amount of time you spend in each of these categories or others. Think about what kind of person you want to be: the one who dreams, or the one who gets lost in someone else's dream. Now, try and decode which dream killers you need to rid yourself of (or at least cut in half) before they suck the life out of you, manipulate you, and keep you from dreaming the dreams God has for you.

- Media
- Music
- Dumbed-down reading
- Internet

THE MEDIA IS STEALING THE HOURS OF YOUR LIFE THAT YOU SPEND WATCHING THEIR STUFF. INSTEAD OF BEING A DREAMER AND CHANGING THE WORLD, YOU ARE WATCHING SOMEONE ELSE'S DREAM AND BEING ENTERTAINED BY IT.

CHAPTER 5

CULTURE ZOMBIES

It's been said that 98 percent of our culture are followers of culture and only 2 percent are shapers of culture. Ninety-eight percent of people take their cues from an advertiser or a media machine as far as what they should do with their time and money, and what they should wear. Essentially, 98 percent are in a trance. If a band has a new CD coming out on a certain date, that's the date they are going to purchase it. If a network has a certain special, they are going to be there with their popcorn to watch it on that certain night. They are very obedient, tuned-in followers of a culture that is happy to dish out orders.

How can you tell if someone is in that 98 percent? Have you ever heard someone say, *"Did you see that movie trailer? I can't wait until the movie comes out."* That is a culture zombie. They are taking cues from the culture and doing what the culture wants them to do.

"Every Tuesday night I have got to see my TV program. I watch it every week." Another culture zombie doing exactly what the network wants them to do.

"I've got to get my hair cut just like that star! I can't wait get it done!" Another Culture Zombie.

"I've got to have those pants!" Culture Zombie.

"My team has only lost three games this season. I hope they go all the way to the championship." Culture Zombie.

"I've got to have that new CD."

"I've got to see that band when they come in concert."

"There is this new thing happening on my favorite website."

All of these are attitudes and actions of Culture Zombies. Some people are actually proud of the fact that they are enslaved by the culture. They say, "I have never missed an episode." All they are highlighting is the fact that they are manipulated by what the culture tells them to do. Some people will say, "I know every single lyric of every single song they have ever written." "I know every detail about the private and personal life of this artist." All these statements highlight that they don't have a life of their own. They are following someone else's life. Some people feel like they *have to* know everything about the love life of their favorite pop icon. Every time that star held hands or kissed is, of course, being broadcast in every pop magazine.

Culture Zombies are everywhere, walking around like they don't have a brain of their own and being obedient to every command that culture presents to them.

Oh, so you say, "Certainly not me! I make up my own mind. I buy what I want. I do what I want. I watch what I want." But is that really true? There are many more of us who are more subject to the slavery of the culture than we would like to believe.

Let's break it down a little more to see if you are actually a Culture Zombie.

The Dashboard

A dashboard is something like what is on the front on your car where you can see indicators of how low on gas you are and how much you're speeding and so forth. So let's give you some indicators to run through your own mind to see how addicted to the culture you just might be.

Television
- Do you have one in your bedroom?
- Was that your decision or your parents' decision?
- How much TV a day do you watch?
- Are there programs that you can never miss or you will lose your mind?

Every television you have is like a pipeline of garbage from the world coming to flood your mind. When our kids were young, my wife, Katie, and I deliberately decided not to let our kids have TVs in their rooms. All their friends had TVs in their rooms. Man, did they want one. Recently I heard my 17-year-old daughter talking about how she's glad she never had a TV in her room because, that way, she never got addicted to it.

CULTURE ZOMBIES ARE EVERYWHERE, WALKING AROUND LIKE THEY DON'T HAVE A BRAIN OF THEIR OWN AND OBEDIENTLY FOLLOWING EVERY COMMAND THAT CULTURE PRESENTS TO THEM.

What About MP3s?

- Do you have an iPod?
- How many songs do you have on your iPod?
- What types of songs are on your iPod?
- Are the songs massively perverted and worldly—but with a few Christian songs to try and balance them out?
- What attitudes are you picking up from the secular music that you do have?
- What do you know about the personal lives of the people that have written the secular music? If some of them are druggies, Satan-worshipers, or people who have been married four to five times, why would you want them to tell you about life? Psalm 1 says, "Don't listen to the counsel of the wicked." Every time you listen to them sing about their perspective of life, they are "counseling" you and teaching you how to live and what attitudes to have. Why would you want that when they've already failed in their own personal life? It does not matter how popular they are.
- How many hours a day do you listen to music? Are there times in your day that you "have to" listen to music while you are doing homework or something else?
- Do your parents know what is on your iPod? Would you care if your parents knew? Would they be thrilled?
- Better yet, if your grandmother happened to see a print out of all the words of the songs on your iPod, would she suffer from a heart attack?

Again, this is just a dashboard for you to start to rate how much of the world's culture you are swimming in.

Computers

- Do you own a computer personally?
- Do you have one in your home?
- How many hours each day are you on it?

- How many hours each week?
- What kind of sites do you go on and watch or participate in?

Video Games

Video games deserve their own category, given the fact that they have surpassed Hollywood movies in total annual sales.

- How many video games do you own?
- What type of games are they?
- How many hours a week do you play?

Cell Phones

- Do you have a phone?
- How often are you on it playing games?
- Watching media?
- Texting people? Is there any texting that you have done in the last month or so that you would be embarrassed for your parents or grandparents to know about?

The fact here is that these and other media pipelines are drowning a whole generation. I would encourage you to be smarter than the world. All of these things are part of the dream killers we talked about earlier. If you are going to be a Culture Zombie, then that is fine, but if you are going to make a difference in the world, you have to eject yourself out of the 98 percent and into the 2 percent. How do you do that? It's by shutting some of these things off. Don't wait for your mom and dad to tell you, "Hey, quit watching so much TV." A creative person that is going to change the world is going to choose by their own will to stop watching or listening to so much stuff and playing so many games. They are going to conserve their energy so they can make a difference in their world.

Take a moment and fill out this little chart. How many hours each week do you listen to or watch any of the media we talked about? What would your goals be? How much of this dream killer would you like to cut away so you can spend more time dreaming?

Area	Average hours per week you spend on this	How much do you want to cut that down to?
Computers		
Video Games		
Cell Phones		
Dumbed-down reading		

Here are a few more questions that can serve as a dashboard to help you think through these issues.

- How many movie one-liners have you used in the past three months?
- How many quotes from advertisements have rolled off your tongue in the last week?
- How many times have you or some else in your family gotten mad or upset in the middle of a movie or show because someone else in the room made a noise?
- When was the last time you asked and asked them to get something for you or let you watch something because everyone else is doing it?
- Can you quote more lyrics from secular pop songs than you can the Bible?
- Do you have any rules for your TV watching at your house, including how many hours per day? Yes or no?
- If not, are you willing to make some of your own rules so you can get rid of some of the dream killers in your life?
- Do you know more about what is happening with Jamie Lynn Spears than you know about what's going on in your own family?

Are You a Culture Zombie?

If you are still happy being a Culture Zombie, pay no attention to everything we've just talked about. If you don't mind being a slave to what others want you to do, then forget you even read this chapter. But if you want to jump out of the 98 percent and into the 2 percent, it's time to shut down some of these dream killers that are destroying you. You can actually begin influencing your world rather than staying in its trance and allowing it to shape who you are.

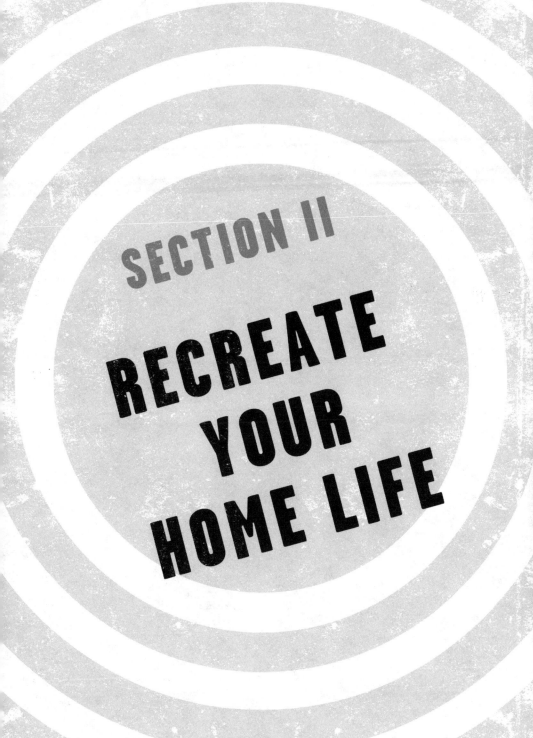

SECTION II

RECREATE YOUR HOME LIFE

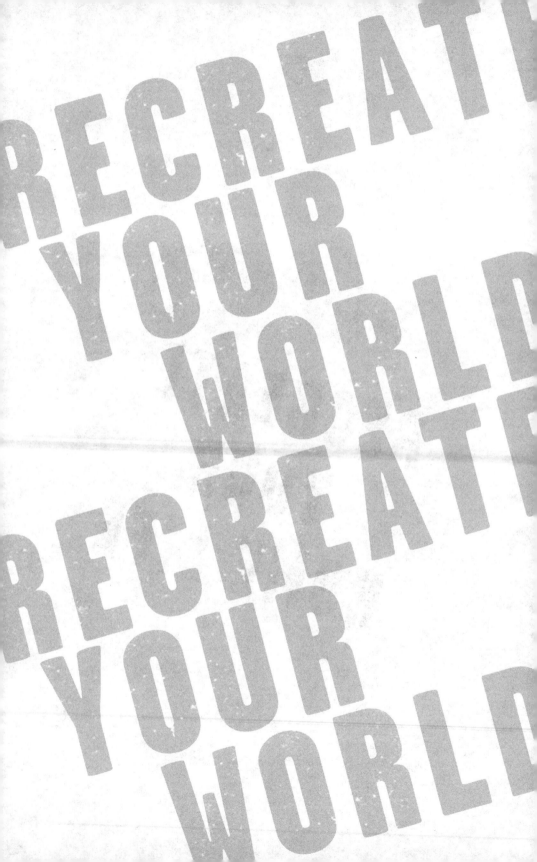

CHAPTER 6

HATE GOING HOME?

If you are like me when I was a teenager, I hated going home. So many young people are like that today. It's just that they don't want to be with their parents. They don't want to be nagged. They hate the tension going on there. They hate when their parents fight with each other. They hate fighting with their parents. They would rather be around other friends or media.

I remember growing up feeling like I was in a prison. My whole home life was a prison camp. I couldn't really tell anyone what it was like. I would do anything to get away from home. Even though I was a lousy sports player, I would still play just so I could dodge home for a couple more hours a day. I would get beat up. The only reason they let me stay on the football team was because they were sure I would quit. I was the smallest guy out there! They cut better players than me. I preferred to be out there getting the snot beat out of me by my peers than go home and feel like I was being emotionally destroyed by my family.

My home life was just an endurance test getting through one day after another after another. If that looks anything like your life, we've got some good news for you here. You can be a part of recreating the whole vibe in your home so that it's somewhere people want to be. Sure, your parents need to get involved. But it's not just your parents; it's you. Your attitude, actions and demeanor can all begin to shift how your parents act and how your brothers and sisters respond.

Are You a Victim?

You might say, "Yeah, really, what can I do? I can't do anything. It's all my parents' responsibility." If that is how you feel, then you are really playing the part of a victim as if to say, "There is nothing about my circumstance that I can do anything about." If you feel that way now about your parents, you are going to feel that way about everybody the rest of your life. You will think, "I'm just a victim. There is nothing I can do." There is plenty that you can do. It's not easy. It's not fun. It might cause your ego to take a few blows, but there *are* things that you can do. Let's brainstorm a little bit, shall we?

Get Rid of the Tension

Most of the tension in our homes is centered around pretty stupid things. They are not big issues. Yeah, big issues come up, but we usually get more exasperated and angry at all the small ones. We get mad about having to take out the garbage, feed the dog, wash dishes, clean our room, pick up our shoes, wash our clothes, or mow the lawn. These are things that really don't make a huge difference. They are just things that we prefer not to do.

I remember so many times in my house growing up, everybody was walking on eggshells hoping that Mom or Dad would not explode, hoping we wouldn't get in trouble for this or that, or even something we didn't even know was wrong. When dealing with tension, whatever the source may be, there are a couple things to remember.

Go Cool Off

Don't try to solve a disagreement while you are flaming mad. You are going to say things you don't mean and regret. You could really wound your parents or siblings. Find some place to cool off and get away. Don't get mad, slam the door and walk out. Just say in a very respectful way, "Mom, Dad, I need to go cool off. Can we come back and talk about this later? Is that alright?" In the heat of the moment you might feel passionate about something, like you really want to get out of there and get done with the conversation right then—but it's hardly ever the right time to do it.

While you are cooling off, remember that if you say something you'll regret, you might win an argument but lose a relationship. Remember that these people that are raising you are called *parents*. They are people. They have feelings that can be hurt too. I think many kids do not believe their parents have feelings that can be hurt just like everyone else. Try to see things from their perspective. Ask yourself the question, "Why is it important for me to be right and get my way in this situation?" Stay cooling off until you can come and deal with the issue without using your emotions. Remember, it's a mark of maturity to have a discussion about really hard issues without getting emotional about it. Just try to separate your emotions from your brain. Use your brain to have that conversation.

Have Fun

Fun can be one alternative to dealing with tension. Think about it. Sometimes I think we get addicted to the tension because we want to win the argument so much. I encourage you, especially when you know it's getting tense, or when *you* are the one that is mad about something that needs to be discussed, think about something funny; it kind of breaks the ice. Remember that at the end of the argument, whoever wins the argument is still going to want to preserve a relationship. Fun

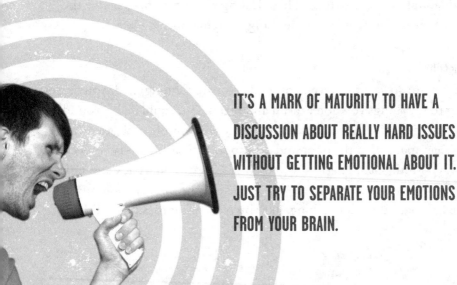

IT'S A MARK OF MATURITY TO HAVE A DISCUSSION ABOUT REALLY HARD ISSUES WITHOUT GETTING EMOTIONAL ABOUT IT. JUST TRY TO SEPARATE YOUR EMOTIONS FROM YOUR BRAIN.

is a great way to preserve a relationship. Think of something fun to watch or do that might break the ice and tension.

This is the beginning. The next couple of chapters are going to help you really and truly get a new start in your home. You'll begin to create a home life that you enjoy and that helps you grow and thrive in your walk with God.

CHAPTER 7

HOW TO GET YOUR PARENTS TO LET YOU DO WHATEVER YOU WANT

Do you think it's possible to actually get your parents to let you do whatever you want to do? Do you really think that's likely? You are probably just reading this chapter out of curiosity because you've tried everything in the book to get your own way and you don't think there's any possible way. But the fact is, *what you're about to read could revolutionize your entire home life*. And you might not get to do whatever you want to do, but you'll definitely get to do a LOT MORE than what you get to do right now.

What I'm talking about is nothing like putting a special trance on your parents, or tying them up and locking them in a room somewhere so that you can do basically everything you want. What I'm about to share with you is a lot more effective than any of that and will have a long-term positive impact on your parents.

The key to getting your parents to let you do whatever you want to do is all tied up in the word "honor." Ephesians 6:1-2 are a parent's favorite verses in the Bible:

> Children, obey your parents because you belong to the Lord, for this is the right thing to do. "Honor your father and mother." This is the first of the Ten Commandments that ends with a promise.

Parents who don't know anything else in the Bible know these words. Parents who don't have anything to do with God and don't even believe in God know these words. Parents have their kids memorizing this verse almost before they can talk (as I did my children). It seems like a parent's secret weapon. But in these few words lies the key to what you are looking for. It starts out, "Children, obey your parents," and then it says, "Honor your father and mother."

What does it really mean to honor? We don't really hear that word much today unless you are in court and you are talking to a judge. But honor is something that you give to someone because of their *position*, not because of the way they treat you, and not just because you happen to like them. You give honor to people because of a title they have or a role they play.

For example, we honor a general in the military even if we don't know him or we've never met him; but he has earned a title and a role that is worthy of our honor and respect. So, even if you are not in the military, you will probably honor him. For example, if the president of the United States comes to your town, they're probably going to have a parade for him; they're going to have people go out and meet him and greet him. Even people of the opposite political party will honor him, even people that don't necessarily agree with his policies in the laws he signs off on. But because we honor this position, we obey those laws. And we may not like the way he does his hair, we may not like the clothes that he wears, we may not like what he does in his personal life. But because he holds that position, he's the president, and we honor him. The same is true with our parents.

God says in His Word that your parents have a position. Out of all the people in the entire world, He chose them to bring you into the world. They were the vehicle that brought you here into the planet, and because of that, they have a position—a title of honor called *parents*. Even the worst parents in the world still have a position because they brought you into the world; they are worthy of your honor. You may not like their rules. You may not like their hair. You may not like the things they say you should do. But God says, "If you honor them, you'll be blessed and you'll have a long life." This is really the only commandment that comes with *a blessing and a promise* to go with it.

How to Honor Your Parents

So, we want to talk about how honoring your parents results in you being able to do whatever you want. It seems like it doesn't even make sense. Hold on tight, you're about to see . . . we're going to talk very practically about what it means to honor.

1. Honor Your Parents by How You Talk *to* Them and by How You Talk *About* Them

This is probably the biggest and most common issue in families across the country: dissing our parents. Sometimes teenagers are even seen cussing at their parents, mumbling, talking about them behind their back, bad-mouthing them to other people, slamming them, and making them look stupid. Of course, the popular media does not help this at all. Most every depiction of a teenager's parents you see in movies and television make parents look like stupid, bumbling fools that are mocked openly.

So the first very practical thing we can do is honor them by what we say to them, how we respond to them: We hold our tongue even though we are angry; we're not led by our emotions at the moment, but we're led by *honor* (there's that word again). How we talk about them matters. I would encourage you to think about trying this: Do not let one negative thing about your parents come out of your mouth, even though you might be with a group of friends where everyone else is talking about how bad their parents are.

We honor our parents by how we talk about them, what we say about them, and what we say to their face. It doesn't mean that we have to go around and tell everyone that we have the best parents in the world, but just don't let anything dishonorable or disrespectful come out of your mouth either in their presence or to their back. If you really need to talk about some things your parents are doing to you, the appropriate place to do that is with your pastor, youth pastor, or counselor at school. But just talking to your friends about it so that you can all just lick each other's wounds and have a pity-party and compare who's parents are worse doesn't help you and it doesn't invite the blessings of God on your life because you're not honoring them.

2. Honor Your Parents by Obeying Them

The Scriptures say, "Children, obey your parents," and the only reason to disobey them is if they tell you to do something that *directly contradicts* the Bible—like if they asked you to sell drugs or to be a prostitute. Well, of course, then you'd need to go to the police and to your pastor or other leaders in your life that would help you walk through that. Most of the things our parents want us to do aren't illegal; they're just things we don't want to do, like taking out the garbage, mowing the lawn, and being home on time.

We honor our parents by obeying them. In fact, we honor them by obeying them the *first time* without having to have them hammer us again and again and again. Let me tell you what happens as you begin to do what they ask you to do the very first time: It creates trust. It creates confidence in them. They're thinking, *Wow, she's really matured/he's really grown up. I barely whispered that rule or that request and they did it the first time.* And it makes them start perceiving you as more responsible and ready to handle more responsibility. And they think that maybe you can make some of your own decisions.

It seems like a paradox—"How could obeying them make them feel like they want to let me make some of my own decisions?" Well, because of the trust—trust is big. Every relationship is built on trust. You don't get trust automatically; you have to earn trust. The way you earn trust is every single time they ask you to do something, BAM! There you are and you do it. The more you do it, the more trust you have, and so the more likely they are to say, "So why don't *you* make a decision about what you *want to do* this time?"

I would make a goal for both today and this week, saying, "Okay, this week every single thing they ask me to do, I am going to do it the very first time they ask." Be careful, because you might actually cause your parents to pass out. They might actually freak out and go into a coma, and then, of course, when they're in a coma, you will get to do

TRUST CREATES FREEDOM. OVER TIME, YOUR PARENTS WILL BE MORE OPEN TO LETTING YOU MAKE MORE DECISIONS FOR YOURSELF BECAUSE YOU'VE PROVEN TO THEM THAT YOU ARE RESPONSIBLE.

whatever you want to do. They'll be so shocked by your obedience that they might end up in the hospital.

3. Honor Your Parents by Offering to Do Things

Okay, you might think this would be leading you down the path of slavery, but actually it is leading down the path of freedom. When you *offer* to do things for them, you go the extra mile. They didn't *ask* you to clean the kitchen but you did. They asked you to do the dishes, but you *also* swept the floor. You go to your dad and say, "Hey, Dad, after I mow the lawn this week how about I wash your truck?" Of course, the first thing your parents are going to do is say, "Who are you and what have you done to my child? Have aliens taken over my kids?" because they'll be so amazed that so much desire from you is coming their way— a desire to serve, a desire to do not just whatever you want, but you're wanting to lighten their load.

Talk about creating trust; this builds massive trust, and, congratulations, you have just aspired to a whole new level of relationship. You've just become the person that they, in their wildest dreams, could never conceive of. They may say, "My kids are actually doing this? They're 14 and 15 and they're offering to do things like this?" If you are able to drive, and you offer to take your younger siblings to school or on other outings, then you are having a servant's heart (like Jesus had). And by becoming a servant, you actually *gain access to freedom.*

After doing the last three, you will begin to create trust. And trust creates freedom. Because they trust you, they'll say, "Well, why don't you make that decision." And you'll find them allowing you more and more. They're not going to allow you everything all of a sudden, but they will become more open to letting you make more decisions for yourself. You'll begin to have more say over your time, your money, and what you do with your life because there's a sense of confidence; they're not wondering if you're going to go out there and be some wild, rebellious young person. You've proven to them that you're responsible, and *that* creates a path to freedom and opportunity for you to make a lot more of your own decisions.

How Do You Honor Your Parents When It's Really Hard?

Some of you may be in a situation like I was growing up, where there is abuse in the home and horrible words exchanged. Things were planted in my mind that I would never forget. Like when I was 13, my mom told me, "Why don't you do me a favor and kill yourself." Maybe you've been in a situation like that where hurtful words or actions have taken place. Maybe you don't know your mom or dad very well and you feel like it's just impossible. Remember, we honor not because of what they have or have not done, *but because of the position that God gave them.* They are your mom and your dad. No one else can be your mom or dad.

The only way to honor those who appear to have done things that are not honorable is to *forgive.* That's right: forgive. I know it's a hard word to hear because if they have done something that has hurt you they deserve to have misery, right? They deserve for you to be mad at them. At least from your perspective you feel like they deserve it. The only way to honor them is by choosing to forgive. In Ephesians 4:31-32 it says, "Get rid of all bitterness, rage, anger, harsh words, and slander, as well as all types of evil behavior. Instead, be kind to each other, tenderhearted, forgiving one another, just as God through Christ has forgiven you." Our job is to take the most hurtful things and, even though you don't feel like forgiving, you choose to forgive.

No one ever wakes up one day and says, "Wow, I really feel like forgiving this person." You'll never feel like it. You *choose* to do it. Why? *Because Jesus forgave you.* He forgave me, so I had to forgive my mom and dad. I had to forgive them for not being there for me. Forgive them for not pouring into me like I wished so desperately they would have when I was younger. I had to forgive them for the horrible things that were said and done when I was younger. By doing that, Jesus truly puts an overwhelming forgiveness and love in your heart for them. You *can* choose to honor them.

Remember, your unforgiveness does not hurt them; it hurts you. It's like a weight on your shoulders. It's like a cancer rotting in your heart. It gets worse and worse. It does not harm them. *It harms you.* By choosing to forgive, you are actually helping yourself. I want to encourage you to find somebody that you can pray with if you have a situation like this in your home. It could be a pastor, youth pastor, or friend. Ask them, "Hey, will you pray with me as I'm walking through this forgiveness?" Let God put forgiveness in your heart so that every time you get angry or want to get angry at them for the same things, you'll say, "No, *this isn't who I am*; I am forgiven, so I will forgive." Instead of rewinding all those horrible memories back through your mind, you bring up that Scripture and say, "Okay, I'm going to keep forgiveness in my heart. I'm going to forgive 70 times 7 like Jesus said." As a result, you will walk in freedom and you will be able to honor your parents.

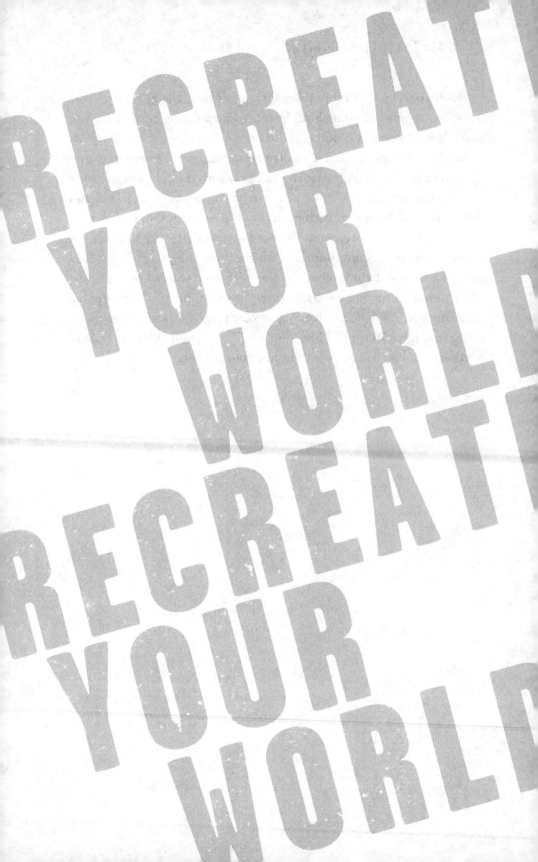

CHAPTER 8

BREAKING THROUGH THE INVISIBLE WALL

I don't know. . ." All too often, that is the only thing we know to say when our parents ask us any questions like, "What do you want to eat? Where do you want to go? What do you want to be when you grow up? What do you want to do tonight? How do you feel about the presidential candidates? How do you feel about global warming? What is your favorite color?" From intense issues to simple issues, it seems like the most common answer from a teen in America is, "Uh . . . I don't know." It is an indicator that a wall has been built up between so many teens and their parents.

No matter who you are, all of us crave relationships. We want to be close to people. We may not act like it sometimes, but we were born for relationships. We long for relationships. We need relationships. The very first people that God gave you to be close to are your parents. Often, at the very moment you don't feel like talking to them about *that one issue*, they ask about it and you say, "I don't know." Even in those moments, there is a drive and a craving deep inside that's driving us toward some kind of relationship.

So many young people say, "I just don't feel close to my parents." What do they mean by that? They certainly live under the same roof and sometimes eat together. They are really saying, "There is a wall between me and my parents. *I'm not relationally close to them*." "I don't think they understand me." "I don't think they know me." They might even say things like, "You don't even know me!" It's kind of a vicious circle. Your parents don't know you because you keep saying, "I don't know." They want to get to know you but that is your most common answer.

It might be a form of payback like, *I don't like what you did to me, so I'm not going to let you have a chance to get inside my heart*. You may not ever *say* that. You just feel it.

There are a lot of lonely people living under the same roof—a family living all together, but all so alone at the same time. What a tragedy! Here we have a group of people all terribly lonely, yet all craving a relationship, saying, "I don't know" when asked a question. Part of the problem is because we are busy. You have school, homework, sports, cheerleading, or other activities. Mom and Dad are also busy. So we are all busy people craving relationships. With nowhere else to find them, we go online and get 5,000 "friends" on our MySpace whom we don't feel any closer to just because they populate our friends list. We are still lonely with 5,000 "friends."

Let's talk about what you can do to break through some of the invisible walls and begin to build a real relationship.

1. Listen to Mom and Dad

I know you have been told this a million times. But I want you to understand that there is a principle here. James 1:19 tells us, "Understand this, my dear brothers and sisters: You must all be quick to listen, slow to speak, and slow to get angry." This means that instead of wanting to be heard, we should seek to hear someone else first. If you start thinking, "I want to really listen to their perspective on life, or in this issue or argument," things will begin to shift. After you listen and listen and listen, it's almost like magic—something will happen. They will begin to want to listen to you.

I know you don't believe me right now because you are thinking that your parents never want to listen to you. But when you begin to listen to them, *they won't be able to help but listen back*. Something happens in almost all humans. It's called *reciprocity*—a big word with a cool meaning. It's what is built inside of human beings that make them feel obligated to listen back. It's the same thing that makes you want to ask, "How are *you* doing?" when someone asks you first. If you really listen with earnestness, look at them in the eye, and reflect on what they are saying—whether it's for 5, 15 or 60 minutes—then at some point they are going to say, "Well, what do *you* think about this?" There is your chance to voice your opinion. If you're caring about what they say, then, eventually, the person will feel like, "Wow! You listened to me—I sort of owe it to you." That is exactly what you've been waiting for them to feel.

Start by asking your parents some questions. Ask them how they grew up and what was important to them. What were your parents' biggest challenges? What were they like when they were your age? Ask them questions and get them talking to you and really listen to them. (Fake listening doesn't count. It only makes you 15 minutes older and none the wiser.) There is so much about our own parents that we don't really understand, like their background, how they were raised, or the struggles they went through. At first they might say, "I don't know. I don't know." But that's probably because they're busy. Keep asking questions and they will talk.

Another thing to do is take your earphones out, turn down the music, turn off the computer. Get away from all of that for a little while. You are listening to Mom and Dad. Don't have your music blasting in your eardrum while you are eating or riding in the car. Take every opportunity you can to listen and let them talk. Don't take every waking moment to be on the computer when you are at home. *Make* some time to ask ques-

WHEN YOU LISTEN TO YOUR PARENTS, IT'S ALMOST LIKE MAGIC—SOMETHING WILL HAPPEN. THEY WON'T BE ABLE TO HELP BUT LISTEN BACK.

tions and they will listen. Again, the point is, when you listen to them, not only do they feel obligated to listen back to you, but as you listen it draws their heart back towards you. The very thing we crave is relationships. The answer is found when we *listen*; their heart will be drawn to yours as you communicate with them. A miracle happens when you listen. Your heart is opened and endeared to the person you are listening to.

2. Cut Them a Break

Too often, when parents realize they are doing something wrong, they try to make it up to their kids by talking to them, taking them somewhere, or spending time with them. Sometimes that infuriates the kid even more. Picture a person crossing their arms, responding with, "I don't know . . . You can't buy my love." It's like you're stuck in a stalemate; you can't go backward or forward. Give them a break! Your parents are not perfect either. Hopefully if you begin to listen to them you will see some of the imperfections, and challenges, and hurts they face in their life. Instead of just stonewalling them with, "I don't know," tell them what you are really feeling. Why are you even saying, "I don't know"? You might even introduce it with saying, "Listen, I really don't want to answer that question, but could I tell you how I'm really feeling?" Many times that honesty can mark the beginning of a very helpful conversation.

3. Breaking Through the Invisible Wall

Think about some of the things that you have done that have not been so positive, and about what could have possibly gone better. Take a long, hard look in the mirror and ask, "Is there anything that I could have done differently in this situation or relationship? Is there anything that I need to ask them to forgive me for?" I know that it's hard because most kids think that parents are wrong. Being open to forgiveness is actually a sign of maturity. I remember when I had to forgive my mom. I had so many awful memories from when I was growing up of the horrible things she said and did to me. But then the Lord began to speak to my heart: "You know, Ron, you were not a perfect kid either. You need to ask her to forgive you because you did a lot of stupid and hurtful things to her." Many times when you go in with that humble disposition that says, "I am so sorry because I know that I was *part of the problem,*" that draws their heart back towards you. It takes a real man or a real woman to admit that they were wrong and ask for forgiveness—even if you feel like they were way guiltier than you. Start with that. Sincerely ask for forgiveness for specific things. You will be amazed at how the invisible wall begins to collapse and crumble.

4. God Will Provide

Maybe you don't live anywhere near your parents. Maybe one of your parents is gone. Maybe you've never even met one of them. Maybe you feel bitter or mad because you're so far away. Maybe your parents are married, living with you, but no matter what you do, you can't seem to break the invisible wall. I just want to encourage you with these words: *God will provide.* The Word says, "He is a father to the fatherless; He is a friend to widows and orphans" (Deuteronomy 10:18).

What does that mean? It means that you might *feel* like an orphan because your parents are just so far from you. You might not have a real relationship with them. You might *feel* fatherless because your dad is not around. The Bible says that God will be that father and He will be a father *to you.* I can tell you about people that I know who have never met their dad because he was an alcoholic who left when they were a child. These same people say that, in a very real way, "God was my father all throughout my teenage years. I could go to Him for anything." Besides that, God will provide other people from church or other places who can be a father or a mother to you—to pour into you, and love on you, to dote on you, and to tell you how *proud* of you they are. Don't give up. God has not given up on you. Don't you dare give up on God. He is going to take care of you. Ultimately, He is the one who meets our needs—not our mom and dad.

SECTION III

RECREATE YOUR WORLD

CHAPTER 9

DREAMERS ALWAYS WIN (THE CULTURE WAR)

We are in a war, whether we like it or not. Our culture is shaping our generation, and we have to fight to get the right values into the culture. It is a battle of ideas. It is a battle of dreams. *Whoever dreams the most compelling dream wins the culture war.* This is where we as believers must step into the national conversation of ideas.

You don't have to look far to see that most of the people who shape our culture today don't have much regard for the Bible or for the values found in the Bible. In fact, most people who are in the 2 percent are totally opposed to the values in the Bible. It seems like they have done everything in their power to make normal the very things that God says He hates in the Bible. To accomplish this, they have built businesses without moral values for the purpose of selling stuff to young people, just for the sake of making money. Those dreams are becoming a reality.

It may not be that everyone is actually thinking, *We want to change the value system of our country*, but the media and products they make are achieving that. It may just be that the 2 percent are so interested in making money that they've decided there's *no right or wrong way* to do that. "Let's just make anything we can get people to buy" sounds fair enough to them.

Either way, we become the victims. When we hear a song 500 times about how to treat a woman indecently, or that the way to deal with a problem when you're mad is to shoot somebody, it has an undeniably negative effect on the listener. The current shapers of culture have successfully dreamed a dream and then wooed the majority of the young generation to march to the beat.

Be a Problem Solver

It's not just one person or one organization or corporation that is shaping the culture. We mentioned Viacom earlier, but there are five major communication companies that control most of the movies and music of the world. They are AOL Time Warner, Disney, Bertelsmann, News Corporation and Viacom.[1] These media empires, while in competition with each other for the majority market share, continue to drag down our generation.

In many ways, they've won. They've won the culture war. They have dominated the culture. And they've done it by dreaming big and incorporating young people into their dream. So now it's time for us to dream.

What could we do as God-fearing citizens to help shape our culture? The task seams terrifying, almost impossible. It also seems impossible to create a godly culture that overwhelms, rather than the world's culture. But the fact is that we can create a culture in our family, in our church and in our community that is stronger than the world's culture if we are proactive about it.

Now we have another *seemingly impossible* task. So where do we start? We need to dream a big dream about which part of the culture we want to affect and then roll up our sleeves. We need to be smart about how we approach it. Consider Rudy Giuliani in New York City. He made some significant progress in ridding the city of pornography, but not in the way you might think. The many porn shops in the city were driving away tourism. Giuliani knew that he could not use "morality" as grounds for removing them, because people would cry "freedom of speech." So he got a law passed that said there will be no porn shops within 500 feet of a school or within 1,000 feet of a place of worship. Well, there are 16,000 schools in New York City and thousands of churches and synagogues. With one signature, he shut down thousands of triple-X porn distribution centers!

We need to be *smart* about how we mean to change culture and make it better for our generation. We need to make sure that as believers we are not finger pointers. The pointed finger of condemnation is usually what the world thinks of when it thinks of Christians. So we need to come to the table with creative ideas that help bring solutions. We need to do more than preach; we need to be *problem-solvers.*

Your Dream Is Your Voice

If we want to have a voice that's able to redirect our culture and our nation, we can't just come with problems; we have to come with solutions, with creative ways of compelling young people and industry to rally around and believe that we all can make a difference.

WE CAN CREATE A CULTURE IN
OUR FAMILY, IN OUR CHURCH AND IN
OUR COMMUNITY THAT IS STRONGER
THAN THE WORLD'S CULTURE IF WE
ARE PROACTIVE ABOUT IT.

I was contacted by the executive of a large perfume company, who had seen the cover of a *New York Times* article on this young generation.[2] The article had a picture of young people on their knees giving their heart to Jesus.

It talked about the battle that's going on with this generation, and I was interviewed about it. The executive who called me had an idea of doing a perfume that would inspire young people to be pure and not stoop to seeking to be sexy and show skin. After much research, they found that young people (not just Christians) would be *just as likely* to buy a fragrance that helped them to aspire to be pure as they would to be sexy and worldly. So we are now walking down that path together with them. Think about marketers with brands competing against each other to see who has the most virtuous fragrance! That is an example of beginning to shape culture in a major way.

We can't just say we don't like this or we want such-and-such to be different; we've got to be the ones that dream a new dream for our friends who are on drugs, the girls that are pregnant. Let's get a vision of how we can help teens deal with other issues. If we don't like our friends hanging out at a certain place in town, we've got to suggest a place for them to hang out that's wholesome and that's going to create a fun environment.

People follow dreams, not directives. People won't do what they are told to do or what they are supposed to do. But they will do what they are inspired and compelled to do. Dreamers are the ones who know how to compel them to follow.

So now it's time to dream a dream for the kids you don't know, the kids who aren't in your family, the kids you may never meet. Even though you don't know all of them, they will benefit from your dream. The people who mastermind the marketing at MTV and Victoria's Secret never meet all the people they affect (and so they think that it doesn't really hurt anybody). They are affecting millions. They dream a dream for the sake of money and market share. But we have a more noble cause. We dream a dream on behalf of the future of our nation and the hearts of a whole generation.

Go to http://battlecry.com/pages/chapter21.php to see what happened when 1,000 teen dreamers gathered in Times Square.

CHAPTER 10

PARALYZED BY THE ORDINARY

I'm afraid that too many of us find ourselves in church every week being the very embodiment of the title of this chapter. We see things that are "ordinary" and we think that's just the way it's supposed to be. Status quo is comfortable; status quo is what seems acceptable. The status quo keeps us from ruffling feathers because Christians don't want to ruffle anybody's feathers. It seems like every time we do anything greater than the status quo, we get a slap on the wrist by the world, accusing us of being "intolerant." And so that keeps us to ourselves.

I wonder if we have been so programmed by what we call "normal American culture" that we think we're supposed to find a way to just survive in the midst of it rather then be a change agent in it?

Hypnotized by the Ordinary

Dude, I have all these dreams, but I think I'd rather just chill here on my couch for a while like everyone else. Let me just prop my feet up . . . There, that's better—nice and comfortable.

We see in the passage at the end of John (see chapter 21) that Peter, after following Jesus around for three years, had seen all the miracles and heard all the parables. Peter was right there when Jesus died, he was the first to discover that He rose from the dead, and he witnessed, front and center, as Jesus ascended into heaven. After seeing all this, now Peter was pondering what he was going to do with his life. He was wondering what to do next *after he had heard the Great Commission* (see Matthew 28:18-20). His suggestion to his friends was, "I'm going fishing"; others said, "We will go with you." So in spite of all the miracles, in spite of all the life-changing encounters that Peter had experienced, he still had this lingering thought of what "a normal life" was. Normal life was fishing; it's what he knew. He was going to go back to what he knew; he was going to go back to the *comfort of the known*. He was content to go back to not ruffling anybody's feathers. He was going to stay in the safe zone.

We look at the ordinary as the way things are *supposed to be*. Our equilibrium as humans is constantly geared toward, "Let's go back to what we know; let's go back to the way it used to be; let's go back to what's familiar." So, if we were familiar with or used to a culture that is constantly criticizing Christian values, that constantly parades sex in front of our eyes as if it were something worthless, then we might just start to think it's normal.

Once in a while, there is a shocking interruption that we just can't believe happened, like Janet Jackson's "wardrobe malfunction" during the Super Bowl game, or Madonna and Britney Spears's kiss; but then we sort of go back to the normal, even if normal gets a little bit worse. The fact is, those types of events make what is currently normal take another step down. All of a sudden, what people will accept is much lower as a whole, since it's not as bad as flashing a breast during a supposed family time of TV viewing, or watching the same-sex, open-mouth kiss of two celebrities.[1]

If we get into a sort of trance with the ordinary, then that's all we'll accept. Literally, what we see is what we get. If we stay focused on what we think is normal, that becomes what we are willing to tolerate. Even though we know it is destroying our entire generation, we accept it as normal. As humans, our nature is to be absorbed into the 98 percent, as followers of culture. It's pretty easy and painless to kind of roll with what everyone else is doing. But the second we jump on the bandwagon with the masses, our power to affect the culture is ripped away.

Instead of accepting life how it is and allowing it to hypnotize us into mediocrity, we must start dreaming about *what could be*. What is the dream that God is calling us to dream? What do we really want to be influenced by? Focusing on that dream will jolt us out of this trance we're locked into—like a splash of ice-cold water to the face.

When We Legitimize the Ordinary

Yeah man, it's legit. It's just the way things are. I'm normal, you're normal—no big deal . . .

We often say to ourselves, "I'm an ordinary Christian. I go to youth group; I'm a pretty good person; I don't kill anybody; I don't lie that much; I'm like everybody else, even if there are compromises in my life."

So we begin to legitimize the ordinary. "Other people live like this; why would I want to be so radically different from them? Why would I lift my voice to shape my generation? Why should I have to ruffle anybody's feathers? Everybody else is kind of going downstream, so I'll just kind of go with it." We justify the compromises we make while letting the creators of this culture triumph in their quest to dominate our generation. We legitimize our own lack of impact and view the culture we live in as *not really that bad*.

Jesus said that narrow is the way that leads to life, narrow is the path, but wide is the path that leads to destruction (see Matthew 7:13-14). As a result, we lose our idealism. First Corinthians 3:3 says that when we are acting worldly, we are acting like "mere men." We are not supposed to live like *mere men*; we're not supposed to live like everybody else.

As a result, the impact of our lives is minimized because we compare ourselves to the ordinary. Nobody else is saying much about it, so we don't want to rock the boat and allow ourselves to engage in change. As a result, we don't even give birth to new ideas, because we are so concerned about being a part of the ordinary.

IT IS TIME FOR US TO BREAK THE STRANGLEHOLD OF OUR CULTURE. IT IS TIME FOR US TO RISE UP AND SAY, "I'M NOT GOING TO LET THIS GO ON. NOT IN MY GENERATION."

Break Out of the Ordinary

Hey, you! Yeah, I'm talking to you. Do you got all your stuff? 'Cause today we're breaking out of this thing. We've been locked in a bit too long for my taste . . . and it's about time we got out.

Every time we see something that needs to change but do nothing about it, we give up the power of our impact. And every time we give in, we become more addicted and mesmerized by the ordinary. If we see something happen that is horrible, we try to find a million reasons why *we shouldn't be the ones to do it*. We're quick to point out the people who are putting the horrible things in movies or on TV screens, *yet we do not do anything*. Doing nothing legitimizes our culture.

As believers, as followers of Christ, we must open our eyes and realize that for too long we've been in a trance, along with everybody else, addicted to the ordinary. If we don't wake up, we will continue to let the wrong people shape society. They are not afraid to ruffle feathers. Most of the feathers they ruffle are moral feathers, and if we object, they call us narrow-minded prudes.

It's time for us to call these people what they are: *virtue terrorists* who make money by ripping any kind of moral virtue from our culture. We must tear ourselves away from the "trance of the ordinary" and start asking what God wants us to do for our community and nation. It's time for us to rise up and say, "Hey, I'm not going to let this go on. Not in my generation."

It's time for us to break the stranglehold of our culture and use our voices to shape the direction of this nation for our generation and the ones to come. We decide what is "common" lingo and "normal" culture; it's only what we *allow* it to become. Whatever we decide to do is going to sculpt the shape of our culture. Your life is writing your own generation's history as we speak—what will you do with it? It's time to wake up and realize that the direction of this nation and its people is in *our hands*.

Go to http://battlecry.com/pages/chapter22.php for a shocking video illustration of how the culture machine sucks us in and redefines "ordinary" for us.

CHAPTER 11

MAKE SOME NOISE, SOMEBODY

Do you feel the freedom to let your voice be heard? Have you been inspired to dream a dream to make a difference in your family and in your community, in your nation and the world? Please don't go out and start with a banner or bullhorn. Creative noise has to be expressed with art, the expression of our faith. It starts out with a dream. What area do you feel most drawn to rescue people?

Creative Noises in Our Culture

First of all, responding to the world is one of the ways that we can communicate our values even though we take a defensive position. When we see things that go against what we hold to be true values and lifestyles, we need to say something. We can be kind about it, but we can make some noise.

For example, if you see billboards that are perverse, don't allow the images to stay there. What we allow is what becomes normal. What we allow is what the standard becomes. If you see commercials on TV that upset you, make a stand. Say to the television station, "We don't appreciate this programming." Tell your friends at church, "Hey, let's tell these guys that we don't want this garbage." When you see these massive billboards in a mall that are showing women with hardly any clothes on, you take a stand and find out how you can get those images taken down. You don't just protect your eyes; you protect your family's eyes and the eyes of the entire community.

Think about the things you hear on the radio; the things you see on MTV; the things you hear in common speech. Whether your school is teaching a certain lifestyle, or handing out birth control on campus, any and every time we see the values of the Bible trampled, we ought to stand up and say, "Wait a minute; something has gone really wrong here. Is this the kind of lifestyle we really want? Do we really want this kind of community?" Even non-Christians, when you talk about the need to protect your generation and those younger than you in their community, many times they want to do the right thing too.

Your Creative Noise in the Culture

We all need to have a defensive side, but more important is the need to creatively think about how we can use our voices to influence people of all ages in our town. Think about all the different ways you could get them involved, especially with Internet access that gives us so many opportunities to take what used to be a small voice and broadcast it to the world. Blogging is just one of the many ways you can do this. You can choose to start a blog and get people to subscribe to it so that the word spreads virtually around the Internet on issues that you may want people to engage and gather momentum for the purpose of social change.

A Video Post

With the advent of YouTube and GodTube and other Internet sites, you can make videos that are seen worldwide by hundreds of thousands, even millions, of people. Just a few short years ago, this would have been virtually impossible without millions of dollars. Maybe you're really talented at making videos, or you could get some of your friends together and create a blog. Let those creative juices flow, and get what message is burning in your heart into hearts all around the world.

Writing

Whether it's poems or books, you may have a creative gift to express yourself. There are a number of websites that will let you post your writing. One popular site for young writers is www.poetry.com. For the artists, check out www.deviantart.com. Neither of these sites is specifically

WHEN WE SEE THINGS THAT GO AGAINST WHAT WE HOLD TO BE TRUE VALUES AND LIFESTYLES, WE NEED TO SAY SOMETHING. WE CAN BE KIND ABOUT IT, BUT WE CAN MAKE SOME NOISE.

for Christians and can be used as a tool to share your faith. Other options to check out include the Christian Writers Guild at www.christian writersguild.com. Personal Web pages and blogs are other great ways to express thoughts.

Music
Maybe you are talented in music. Whether your heart is just for leading worship, or expressing the ideas that God put inside you, your gift is valuable. I encourage you to get your church involved. Find people who will stand behind you and support you. Then do whatever you can to get the word out. Make a demo. Find places to play. Music is like the international love language. If you can speak life through your music, you will reach hearts that would perhaps never hear it in any other way. If you have a gift inside you, let it come out and do the work that it takes to live out the dreams on your heart.

Board of Education
Another way to use your voice is to get involved in the local school system. You may not realize it, but as a member of the local school board, you have tremendous opportunity to influence what is allowed in the schools, particularly in their libraries and curriculum. Find out when the elections are. Find out when people get nominated. Find out the process of getting elected. Watch it for a few years and see how you can get involved. We want there to be Christian people with biblical morals and values involved in making the decisions about sex education and whether or not condoms should be passed out in the schools to 11-year-olds. You can end up being the stop cap by preventing rude and crude teachings and videos from getting into schools. Not only do you protect your kids, but you protect everyone else's kids as well.

Government
Think about how you can get involved in running for office. This might be in your local city council, or even running for mayor. Remember that getting involved in the government is one way that you can help shape

the culture. We need godly people that will shape our culture. Just like when our country began, everyone can benefit from a wholesome, decent culture. That is only going to happen if concerned people like you and me jump into the fray of shaping this world. Sure it's a risk. Sure it's not comfortable. Sure it's out of line of what you thought you would do. Many people think, "Well, I'm already busy with my career and trying to raise my kids. I don't have time for anything else." But it's going to take people willing to sacrifice in order to shape the culture and protect the kids who don't have godly Christian parents.

Our Real Job

So you can see our real job is to make sure that a fervent passion for God and a strong standard of decency are clearly communicated in our culture. We want to clearly communicate our values in a way that we make creative noise in our culture. If we do it in an appealing way, people will want to be a part of it. We must engage the entertainment world, whether it's good entertainment like *Narnia* and other wholesome films, standing up and supporting that, or whether its seeing some of the destructive entertainment and making some noise saying we are not going to support those sponsors. Let's engage in government either by standing

IT'S GOING TO TAKE PEOPLE WILLING TO SACRIFICE IN ORDER TO SHAPE THE CULTURE AND PROTECT THE KIDS WHO DON'T HAVE GODLY PARENTS.

up for godly, wholesome government leaders or by becoming one of those yourself. We must participate in education, whether it's making noise about the horrible things that are sneaking into our education system or standing up for wholesome teaching like abstinence and sex education so the kids in our schools are getting trained in a wholesome way. It's time to unleash a flood of our poetry, songs, inventions, giftings and ideas. We have all heard the saying "It's time to make some noise" at a ball game or concert. Well, this is the word to the Body of Christ: "It's time to make some noise, somebody!" Let's do it with all our heart in a creative way that compels people to listen.

Go to http://battlecry.com/pages/chapter25.php to see some great examples of teens making creative noise.

CHAPTER 12

REAL-LIFE
SUCCESS
STORIES

As I travel around the country speaking to hundreds of thousands of teenagers each year, it's exciting to see that young people are beginning to jump into the middle of the fight to take their generation back. I have heard some very inspirational stories of young people who have not just sat back and let the culture destroy their peers.

Morality at the Mall

Victoria's Secret was doing what they thought was just another day of business when a group of 30 teenagers showed up. Standing outside the store, the first student went in and asked for the manager. The manager came in to see him, and the student asked, "Sir, would you please take down these posters? They are not good for our generation; they are not good for the guys to see. They make us look at women in all the wrong ways. And it doesn't really give women dignity like they deserve." The manager got mad and kicked him out.

So the second member of the youth group went in and asked to see the manager. The manager came in and the next student said, "Sir, would you please take down your posters? They are destroying our generation, destroying how we look at women." The manager got mad and kicked him out. So, they sent in number three. He, too, asked to see the manager, and the same scenario went down yet again. All 30 members in the youth group made it in, one at a time.

Finally, after the manager had kicked out the last student, the whole youth group went in together and pleaded, "Sir, would you please take down the posters? Don't you know that they are destroying our generation? Don't you care about what you are doing to us?" The whole store suddenly got completely silent and the shoppers froze as they listened to these students. The manager carefully, intentionally walked over and began to take down the posters.

Now, that is an example of some young people who had an idea of a creative way to impact the culture. What they did was not about just protecting themselves, but it was about protecting every kid in their community from having to be exposed to the garbage that Victoria's Secret often displays in their shop windows for all the world to see.

Moving Product off the Shelf

During Christmas break, a youth group from Arizona found out about a group that was selling what they called "pornaments." These were ornaments for a Christmas tree that were actually pornography. We at Teen Mania found out about it and emailed our massive list of young people around the country to find out if they would do something about these sorts of items being sold. Kids started going into stores with little video cameras and confronting the sales people, asking them, "Is there not anything sacred? Not even Christmas anymore?" Some salespeople walked off the job and quit right then and there. Other managers decided to pull the "pornaments" off the shelves on the spot. But then the youth group decided to get smarter and engage the maker of these items that were being sold in stores all across the state of Arizona. The youth group wrote a letter asking the company to cease from selling. The company did pull the item from their inventory, just because *one youth group* took action.[1]

He Was Freeing Slaves Before He Could Drive

Zach Hunter is another young man who, at 15 years old, began to crusade across the country to stop slavery as we know it. In an interview with *Good Morning, America*, his parents talked about how shy he was as a child. Then when he was 12, he started reading books about slavery during Black History month that led him to discover that there are still 27 million slaves today.[2] He went on to start an organization called Loose Change to Loosen Chains, to encourage young people and adults to raise money to send to anti-slavery organizations such as IMJ, Free the Slaves, Child Voice International, Rug Mark and Justice for Children International. He is the global youth spokesperson for Walden Media's Amazing Change campaign. And, at the request of publishers, Zach wrote a book called *Be the Change: Your Guide to Freeing Slaves and Changing the World in 45 Days While Still Going to School.*[3] He then went to some of the biggest meetings here in the U.S. and around the world, including an interview on CCN. (Both interviews can be found on his organization's MySpace site at http://www.myspace.com/lc2lc.) As Zach says, "We need to raise money to do this. We need to stop international slavery and slavery around the world where people by the millions are still enslaved by oppressive regimes."

Teen Becoming Mayor

There is a young man named Michael Sessions in Michigan, who at 16 years old decided to look at the laws to see if there was an age limit on running for a political office. He discovered there was *not an age limit* to run for mayor and decided to run in his town when he was a junior in high school. He got all of his friends out campaigning, even though they were not yet old enough to vote. At first, it was thought of as a joke. But he did not take it as a joke. On election day, Michael Sessions actually won the role of mayor in his town. His senior year of high school was spent in a half-day of school, and running over to take care of his responsibilities as the mayor in the remaining half. In his town, it was only a part-time job. (That's a pretty sweet part-time job right there.)[4]

Jordan Kintner

Before Jordan Kintner went to the Honor Academy during his senior year, God created a revolution in Jordan's heart that caused a revolution at his school. It was nearly the end of his senior year, and he was desperate to make an impact on his school. While God had previously used Jordan and others from his youth group to start a prayer meeting on campus, Jordan was still not satisfied. So one day as he sat in class, he prayed, "God, if You could use me to touch this school for You, do it. Help me, Father, to make an impact on my class for You that will be remembered."

Only a few minutes after he prayed this prayer, a girl from the student body government came up and asked him if he would speak at his class's Baccalaureate service, which would be held during the same week as graduation. Jordan's heart jumped when the girl told him that he could speak on any topic.

A few months later, the Baccalaureate service arrived. During the presentation, Jordan told the entire group of 150 to 200 people in attendance that only a relationship with Jesus Christ would satisfy the longings of their hearts. He pleaded with those present to come and talk with him and asked them to not let his words just be a message, but to let it change their lives.

Jordan states, "This is something that I did in my teenage life that I suppose you could call 'dramatic' for God, but in all honesty I don't see it that way. I was just trying to make a difference in my school."[5]

Jesus Cookies

Brianna Keleher is another teen who is making a difference. In September 2006, Brianna went to an Acquire the Fire event held in Amherst, Massachusetts. At one point during the session, a Compassion International advertisement came on that immediately grabbed her attention. When the opportunity came, Brianna went over to the Compassion International booth, and in a short while she was the proud sponsor of a child in Lima, Peru.

Brianna knew that there were a lot of students at her school who also wanted to help but who wouldn't take the step of sponsoring a child for themselves. So she came up with an idea to sell "Jesus Cookies" in her class, with all of the proceeds going toward Compassion International.

DON'T BE AFRAID TO JUMP INTO THE MIDDLE OF THE FIGHT TO TAKE YOUR GENERATION BACK!

In three days, Brianna started selling the cookies, and from the beginning of October until the beginning of June, she was known as the "Cookie Lady." The Jesus cookies were made by kids, bought by kids, and the proceeds went to a kid. Brianna found that selling the cookies also gave her a great opportunity to talk with students about what Compassion International stands for. Today, she is still known as the Cookie Lady at her school.[6]

I hope that these stories inspire you. I hope they excite you. I hope they thrill and compel you to action.

Go to http://battlecry.com/pages/chapter26.php to hear directly from teens who are changing their generation.

CHAPTER 13

ARE WE NOT DREAMERS?

And after this, I will pour out my spirit on all flesh. Your sons and daughters will prophecy and your old men will dream dreams.

JOEL 2:28

Dreamers own us. They always have. Throughout history, those who dream the most compelling dreams are the ones who earn the following of the masses. Whether the dreamer is a political candidate who sweeps the elections or a general who compels men to follow him, those who have cast their dream with a captivating air have claimed the hearts and lives of the general population.

Who are some of those dreamers? How about Bill Gates? He dreams about software; and if you're typing on a PC (as I am, writing this chapter today), you are participating in his dream (while he makes money, of course). What about Steve Jobs of Apple? Do you own an iPod? Every time you turn it on you are part of his dream. Every time you download a song or podcast on iTunes, you enlarge his dream! These are two dreamers who have shaped our culture, indeed, our everyday lives, in a very real way. Who else? What about Martin Luther King, Jr.? Who can forget his resounding words, "I have a dream . . ."? We as a society are the ones who benefit from his dream for equality among the races. He ignited a movement of morality that made us all better human beings. But where are the other dreamers who can make us better as a whole today? Where are the dreamers who can dream a dream to help people, rather than just sell something to them? Our country was founded by such dreamers, so where have they all gone?

Where are the people of God in the 2 percent? *Can we not dream?* Can we not conceive ideas to touch, rescue and affect the masses? Why is it that today, most of the dreamers who control culture are dreaming dreams that benefit only themselves?

Whether it is lyricists carefully crafting words of how to shoot an enemy to solve a problem or take advantage of young girls sexually, or makers of certain video games that teach us to blow people away, these creators of culture have been successful in transferring the wrong values into hearts and minds of a great deal of our generation.

We did not ask for this garbage.

Think about it. Most of the things that shape us in this culture were sold to us. First, the ads spawned a desire in us for the product. If we had never seen the ad or talked to a friend who saw the ad, we would have never known that we *needed* what the ad sold. Then merchandisers made it very easy to access and get our hands on what was advertised. The culture machine is not just media, it is stuff—stuff to see, stuff to watch, stuff to go to, stuff to wear, stuff to give, stuff to drink, stuff that makes you pretty, stuff that makes you cool, stuff that makes you popular, stuff that makes you sexy, stuff that is fun to do, stuff that is adventurous, stuff that will live your life for you so you don't have to go anywhere or do anything. Our lives are filled with *stuff*.

The problem arises when this stuff actually hurts us because our vision becomes blurry as we try and figure out what is moral and what isn't, or when we don't even realize that we're getting addicted to stuff. We talked about the thousands of studies that have proven that seeing violence makes people more violent. Yet these creative geniuses use their creativity to figure out how to make the blood splatter more realistic on the screen in order to sell more product. They know it harms young people, damaging us long-term into adulthood, but they make it anyway. I say they are terrorists. *Virtue terrorists.* They are giving us candy with poison in it and laughing all the way to the bank.

Consider sex in media. Its only use is to sell more stuff and get increased ratings (to sell more stuff). Soft-core porn and sexual references are constantly grazing the screen, whether during regular family hour (averaging 6.7 times per hour)[1] or on MTV (up to 3,000 times per week).[2] All of this is done to make money. They say the sexual content does not affect young people, but there are a number of studies that prove what people with common sense have known for a long time: it does indeed affect us. In fact, the Rand Corporation says that kids exposed to sexual lyrics and media programming are *two times as likely* to get involved sexually as those who are not exposed to it. They are two times as likely to have sex as a teen, catch a disease or get pregnant.[3] Some of these teens will never be able to have children; some will live in pain for the rest of their lives; and some will even die of a sexually transmitted disease, all because someone wanted to make money. Can you see why I call them virtue terrorists? They are ripping any kind of moral virtue from our generation in the name of economic freedom.

They keep dreaming of new *stuff* to see if they can generate an appetite for it. They are stooping to more extreme levels of depravity, hoping to rise above the noise made by the scores of products sold to teens. Think of the filmmaker who depicted 12-year-old Dakota Fanning being raped in a movie titled *Hounddog*.[4] They made the movie, and then brought it to the Sundance Film Festival and tried to sell it to movie distributors. It got a lot of media attention, but thankfully not one chose to distribute it yet. But what does it say about us as a society that they thought they might be able to market it here?

What the Dreamers Know

Why do you think that Bill Gates only lets his own kids on the Internet for 45 minutes a day?[5] Do you suppose he's trying to keep them from becoming part of the 98 percent who follow culture? Do you think he perceives the addictive nature of entertainment on the Internet? Maybe that is why he refuses to allow his kids to get sucked into what he made effortless for the masses to access. How about Steven Spielberg and Tom Cruise, who

ARE WE NOT DREAMERS? CAN WE NOT HAVE A VOICE IN SHAPING THE CULTURE OF THE ENTIRE NATION SO THAT OUR VALUES ARE WINSOME AND COMPELLING?

will not permit their children to watch more than one hour of TV each day?[6] What do they know about television that we don't? Are they making sure their kids don't become Culture Zombies? They themselves are not part of this 98 percent, and they don't want their kids to be a part of it.

When we think of the 2 percent who lead our culture, we are forced to ask ourselves, *Are we not dreamers?* Are the only people who can engage the interest of our generation perverted, money-grabbing dirtbags? Can we not dream a different dream for our peers and for all kids in our communities? Cannot the people who follow the Creator of the universe be more creative and compelling than those who have a creative gift but exercise it in a way that hurts people for the purpose of making millions of dollars? Why does it seem that only secular people are part of the 2 percent? Where are the people with godly, Christian morals who are dreaming and shaping this generation? *Are we not dreamers?* Can't we dream a dream for our home that will bless and not destroy, causing our whole family to grow and run after their dreams?

Can we not dream dreams that will protect the hearts and lives of our generation? *Are we not dreamers?* Can we not think bigger, imagine bigger, and work harder so that our youth groups are reaching more than just the same 10 people every Wednesday? *Are we not dreamers?* Can we teach our generation how to become so consumed and enveloped with a passionate culture of fervent Christianity that we fall out of love with the things of the world? *Are we not dreamers?*

Can we not have a voice in shaping the extensive culture of the entire nation so that our values are winsome and compelling? Could dreams provoked by our values actually attract people to our values and to the One who shaped our values, that is, the Lord Himself? That is what this book is about: provoking us all to dream for our family, for our generation, for our church, and for our nation. Now is the time for a new generation of dreamers to arise and unite. It's our choice if we're going to be a part of the 98 percent or the 2 percent. *In what percent will you be?*

Go to http://battlecry.com/pages/chapter2.php to experience a special version of this message and learn what it means to be a dreamer.

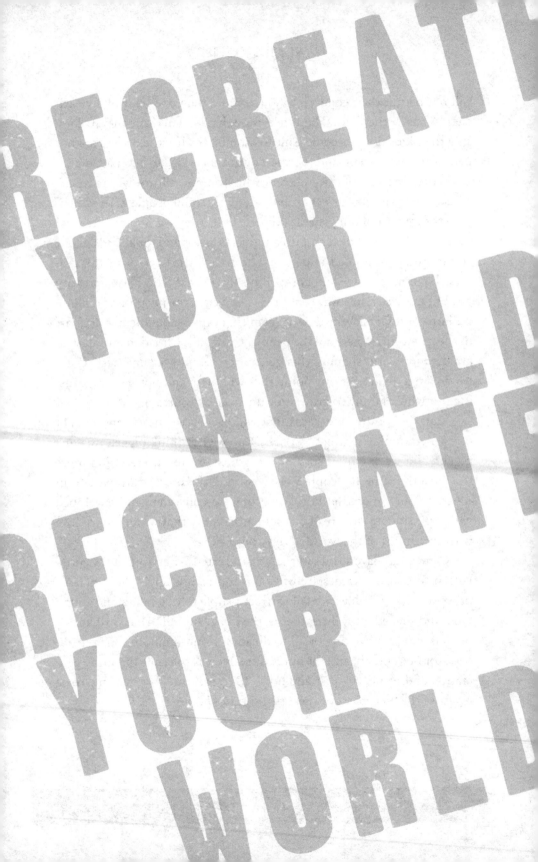

CHAPTER 14

DOUBLE VISION STORIES

We have been talking about dreaming on behalf of your generation. You may not realize this, but there are young people in youth groups all across America who are starting to dream about how they can reach their peers in their schools and community in a massive way. Many youth groups have started doubling and discipling their youth group each year. Youth pastors have caught the vision. Churches are starting to rally around the vision. Young people are getting on fire about having youth groups that are making a huge difference.

As you read the following stories, I hope that you are inspired so that maybe God will spark a dream in your heart for doubling your youth group. I know you might say, "I'm only 14, 15, or 16 . . . What can I do?" You can BE the revolutionary! You can be the one who gets the vision to grow your youth group and spread that vision to your peers as well as to your youth pastors. Don't forget the stories of *real people* like David, Gideon, Mark and Timothy. They were very, very young when they started being used by God. All it takes is *one person* to really get the spark and say, "This could happen in our school. This could happen in our church." Then run like crazy with that vision and God will use you to do something incredible in your own church and youth group.

Doubling and Discipling

Let's look at some churches that have taken the challenge of doubling and discipling and are actually doing the deed! They're reaching kids they have never reached before, and a youth ministry that was previously going nowhere, no matter what they tried, is growing, thriving and exploding both in numbers and in spiritual depth.

Pastor Joshua Shaw: "Emerge" Youth Group (Pennsylvania)

Pastor Joshua Shaw is an amazing youth pastor who has a heart and vision for the kids in his youth group. Pastor Josh's youth group went from 7 to 70 kids in two years. Here is his Double Vision story.

When Pastor Josh decided to pick up and move to become a youth pastor in Pennsylvania, he quickly realized that he was the new guy in town. He took over the previous youth pastor's job, who he referred to as the "Home-town Hero." The previous youth pastor was well known in the community and grew up in the church. But some things came up in this young man's life, and he was asked to step down from his ministry position, which is where Pastor Josh came on the scene.

When Pastor Josh began, everyone thought of him as God's gift to the youth group; everyone loved him. After three months, he realized that he needed a vision and would need God's help to work with youth. He and his wife fasted for a week. Josh told me, "This was no Daniel fast; it was just water." They spent that week seeking, praying, and really seeing what was in their hearts for these kids. They came out of that week with vision and purpose.

They followed the Double Vision curriculum and began casting the vision with the church members. They sat down and looked at people's skills, then targeted those individuals to be a part of the vision and the dream God had given them for the youth group.

Pastor Josh faced a great deal of criticism and skepticism when he first rolled out the plan at a church planning meeting with the leaders. Everyone claimed it wouldn't work and that was that. Pastor Josh did not give up. He basically told them this was the plan, and they could take it or leave it. Eventually, the church members decided to get on board with the vision. Pastor Josh said that God taught him so much through this time.

They went to work on remodeling the youth room, which is now a 2,200 sq. ft. room, which increased attendance. The kids got excited and felt like they were a part of something big.

Pastor Josh's advice to fellow youth pastors is simply this: "Keep your chin down, keep focused, stay close to God and make the job you have now your dream job." He knew that God had called him to do what he was doing, and he kept going with the grace, help and love of the Lord.

Pastor Josh is continuing to disciple the youth, and his push is for attendance to be consistent and to rely on God for growth.

The next examples are direct quotes from and stories about youth ministers who have applied the Double Vision curriculum principles to their youth ministries.

Nancy Harris: 6 to 25 (Oregon)

"Going through Double Vision planning really helped us set a good foundation of leaders passionate about reaching out and mentoring the youth of this generation. The Double Vision curriculum is, by far, the best that we have encountered. DV gave us a step-by-step process on setting a vision, developing a dream and cultivating a plan for our youth ministry. In just 6 months we grew from only 6 teenagers to 25 and, praise God, we're still growing!"

Ben and Heidi Uitenbrobk— 24/7 Youth (Wisconsin)

"Double Vision's been so impacting on our youth ministry. The curriculum helped us put out and develop an impacting vision for our ministry! We've begun to establish, organize and develop a team of leaders to assist our youth. I love how the curriculum shows us exactly how to draw out their talents and teaches us as youth pastors to value them as they help us grow the ministry.

"As we're working on setting goals and developing our mission statement, we've implemented and defined our Core Values. We've also been focusing on Worship and just recently started our own youth worship team. We have a focus on missions and are planning to attend a Global Expeditions missions trip this summer! We've been getting the youth to be a part of the church and involved with outreaches so that when they turn 18, we don't lose them. Our prayer is that even after their time with us, they will stay actively involved in their pursuit of

Christ and pour that passion into the world around them, the same way that we've poured into them."

Donald Simms (California)

"Our deep passion to reach out to today's generation led us to Double Vision. We got the curriculum, did all the workshops and completed the workbooks. We set goals and plans with a vision that we wanted for our ministry and ran with it. We got it around October 2006, and it took until the end of the year to train all of our leaders. We started applying the principles in January 2007.

"God EXPLODED in the hearts of our young people as they became hungry and desperate for the Lord. We saw a big change in their lives; we even did a 'Back to School' event with some local youth pastors and shared with them how the curriculum helped us grow our ministry. Now, most all of them have used Double Vision and are applying it to their youth ministries. The kids were set on fire, excited about the things that God was doing—something you rarely see in many young people today.

"They were starting to get it and began to hide the Word of God in their hearts, applying it in their lives. It's a great program; the material was the best material that we've ever used, and the information is exactly what many youth ministries need. I highly recommend it to anyone who wants to grow their young people and push them closer in their relationship with the Lord!"

Alan Didio (North Carolina)

"The curriculum equipped my leadership with what they can do in order to grow as leaders. They gained vision for the youth. This curriculum opened the leaders' hearts to be positive on what the youth can accomplish. I can say that the youth group has basically doubled since we went through the curriculum about a year ago. We went from 25 to 30 to about 60 to 70. Not only that, but we also have adult leaders who go to schools once a week and talk to teens in ISS (In School Suspension). The multimedia resource that Teen Mania provides helps a lot and makes a difference because they are tools that a small church cannot put together alone. Also, I appreciate that Teen Mania keeps their finger on the polls of what is going on in the world. The information helps the church remain a step ahead of the culture."

Pastor J. D. (Virginia)

Pastor J. D. is 20. He started with 20 kids last year and now has more than 200. He said he did it through *Revolution YM*. (The book and curriculum that thousands of youth groups are using to put a plan together to grow their group. You can order at BattleCry.com.)

He watched the Double Vision DVDs. He said that he and his wife watched the BHAG (Big Harry Annointed Goals) DVD about 15 times and then came up with an idea to build a $15,000 amphitheater to do summertime events in. (He already does a series of summer events called Ablaze and draws hundreds of students during the summer, but sometimes they get cancelled because of rain.)

He used the Double Vision lesson and presented his BHAG to the church board. He said all the board loved it and the vision and they are voting on it this week. This is all taking place in a very rural farm community. This guy is the poster child for Double Vision!!!

Pastor Edwin Pacheco (New York City)

"In 2005, I came across the ministry of Teen Mania and BattleCry on TBN. It was the message of Ron Luce that sparked a desire to see tangible change in my ministry. He shared the frightening fact of what our youth are being faced with . . .

"Since hearing this message we, TRANSFOMED Youth Ministry, have made it our business to reach the youth of our city at any cost. We will not compromise the infallible Word of God, nor will we put any limits on who we minister to. We are living in a desperate time that should cause us to break all the existing 'religious rules' in order to reach a dying generation.

"The BattleCry Double Vision materials helped us to fully define our calling. It's been two years since we adopted the BattleCry approach to ministry, which challenges youth to engage their culture as well as youth groups to become ministries. We have done so and have seen dramatic changes. We have seen teens become fully devoted to Christ, God open doors to go into the public high schools, as well as become influential in citywide ministry . . .

"Today, our youth ministry has grown in number as well as in maturity. We are now challenged with discipling a brand-new group of over 60 youth that have just come into our ministry! We have also launched 20/20 Vision, which is an adopt-a-school initiative from the Coalition of Urban Youth Workers. Over the last year God has also opened the doors to the public schools in our community and we are currently building relationships with school officials.

"As for our efforts locally, we have made our church and community our Jerusalem. There are over 250 youth in our church. Unfortunately, not all are saved. We will not stop our work until each of them is saved, filled with the Holy Spirit, and has become an advocate of their generation. We are in the plans of developing an outreach program that will minister to the homeless, the hungry, and the needy, which will be youth driven. We are also hosting leadership training for youth ministries that are based on the Double Vision resources from BattleCry."

(If you would like more information about TRANSFORMED Youth Ministry and/or Bay Ridge Christian Center, please log on to www.my space.com/transformednyc.)

Bruce Simms— Elev8 Youth Ministry (California)

Bruce Simms had a heart for youth and no formal youth leadership training when his pastor asked him to lead the youth group. He faced some big obstacles right from the get-go. There was no structure to the youth group. Twenty to 25 young people were attending, but only 2 or 3 had a real passion to know God. About half the young people showed up Wednesday nights just to play games and did not even attend the service.

At the very beginning, Bruce was smart enough to realize that after seven years of investment banking, he knew nothing about youth ministry. "I'm the first to admit that when I started I knew nothing about youth ministry. My senior pastor had heard about Teen Mania's Battle-Cry Leadership Summit from a letter sent by Jack Hayford," Bruce says. "I went to the Summit and saw the dynamic ministry that BattleCry is doing and knew I had to bring my young people to Acquire the Fire to be a part."

At the Summit Bruce bought *Revolution YM*—the high-impact guide to youth ministry. Bruce came back with a fervor, passion, and clear-cut ideas on how to Dream, Plan, and Build a purpose-filled and effective youth ministry.

Bruce was ready to change his group. He bought 100 tickets to the Anaheim Acquire the Fire event, did a highly successful fundraiser to cover the cost and had his group invite their friends. When the time for the event rolled around they took 98 teens to the event.

"This event completely, dynamically, fully changed our young people. We knew we couldn't go about doing church the same way, and we knew that there needed to be a separation, a change in how things looked and felt in the youths' minds."

Bruce brought his team back from the event ready to get serious about their ministry. In the fall of 2006, he monitored their growth from 20 to 25 people to 100 in just 3 months! In the fall of 2007, he was looking at attendance and realized they now average 200 different students a week coming to their services!

YOU CAN BE THE REVOLUTIONARY! YOU CAN BE THE ONE WHO GETS THE VISION TO GROW YOUR YOUTH GROUP AND SPREAD THAT VISION TO YOUR PEERS AND YOUR YOUTH PASTOR.

Alex Michel, Church On The Way (Van Nuys, California)

In 2003 Alex Michel was approached by the pastor to become the youth pastor and he accepted. He was at a large church with a small youth ministry and knew a breakthrough needed to happen.

He started with a group of 100 kids that were not unified or open to the teachings from the Bible. He got a copy of *Revolution YM* and was challenged by its uncompromising centrality of the Great Commission in youth ministry. "To what degree does the Great Commission shape the life vision of your kids and your ministry?" he says. "A shotgun might as well have popped out of the books and blasted through my heart. When that challenge came to me, it cut me. 'Lord, we will build this ministry on that concept.' I took the mission statement and said, 'Forget this, I am going to build this and rewrite this onto the Great Commission.'"

This paradigm shift led to a complete overhaul of the foundation of the youth ministry, and began to change the culture and actions of the leadership. Alex realized they had really lost African-Americans, Hispanics, and the mis-fits. In January 2006, being more receptive to a distinct dance culture called "crump" resulted in many salvations and 50 new kids in one service. By mid March attendance increased to 240!

They realized that the culture began to become divided between the crump students and the non-crump students. To incorporate everyone, Pastor Alex spent time with the influencers of the group to get an idea of how to disciple them. Using the principles in *Revolution YM*, he was able to structure different services in such a way that people from the streets feel welcomed and then can also be discipled and become more involved in the church.

But I'm Not a Pastor. What Can I Do?

Maybe you are thinking, "But I'm not a pastor or a youth pastor; I'm just a teenager. What can I do? I guess I don't have a role in all this." What you are is an *advocate*. If you have made it this far in the book, it means that you have a desire that God is stirring in your heart to do something to rescue young people.

Many of these NextGen churches started with an advocate just like you. You can become a champion for the young people in your church and in your community. Go to your youth pastor and say, "I'm here for you. I want you to know that I want to do everything I can to help your ministry to these kids and rescue this generation." It will be a huge encouragement to him or her.

I encourage you to become an advocate and think of what you can do to help your church become a NextGen church. Many of the Next-Gen churches were influenced because somebody (just a normal person like you, and not a church leader) had a heart for kids. They got a *ReCreate* book or a *BattleCry* book or other information about kids. They took it to their pastor, youth pastor and other people in the church and began to woo their hearts toward the young people. I have heard of pastors who then bought one of the books for all the deacons and elders to read. (Some have even purchased books for all the police and the teachers in their town.) They report how their church caught the vision and began to deeply engage young people. As a result, the youth ministry began to grow exponentially. All because of one *advocate*. And now that *advocate* can be you!

An Advocate's Influence

Right now, think about all of the people you influence or could possibly influence. How can you make this challenge personal to you? It's not Ron Luce's challenge or your youth pastor's challenge; it's yours. Think about all of the people you influence at your school or at your job. Think about the people you influence in your Bible study. Think about how you could influence the leaders in your community, whether that is the police chief or the school principal or some other leader. It is amazing how one person with a passion can make a whole world of difference for kids. What about some of the other people you know in other churches in town, and all over the country? We need an army of advocates that bang the drum all over the place, at the same time, if we are to rescue this generation!

As an advocate, the first thing to do is make a list of all the people you could influence because of your relationship with them and all the people that need to be influenced whether you know them well or not right now. Then begin to walk down that list and figure out what you can do to engage them. Next, start going down your list and acting on each item.

Find a way to get books and materials into the hands of those you want to influence. It's one thing for you to share with people; it's another for them to be deeply informed. I encourage you to strategically place books and materials. Ask the people to read what you give them so that you can discuss the contents. Mention that you really want their opinion and thoughts on what they read. As you begin to talk to them, say, "Who else do you think should know about this?" Then you both can brainstorm people they can talk to. Make the list first and then think about what tools you want to have available to begin to influence. You may also want to have your parents invite their friends from your church to go through the six-week small-group course that goes with *ReCreate*. This makes it so easy to watch videos and discuss together all matters concerning your role in reaching this generation.

The doubling and discipling strategy described earlier, on becoming a NextGen church, can be provoked by a committed advocate for young people who refuses to let it be easy for kids in their community to go to hell.

Remember, our job, as members of the kingdom of God, is to go after these kids *more passionately than the world is going after them*. As an advocate, you can provoke that passion and help create a culture in your church that is more powerful than the culture in the world. In this way, once a kid is committed to Christ, he finds his long-lost family—the place where he belongs, the place he can't wait to come back to. As a result, he and others like him are protected from the garbage of the world and are set up to become the champions who will influence their generation for Christ.

Go to http://battlecry.com/pages/chapter20.php to see the story of how a church saw its youth group grow from 20 to 200 teens.

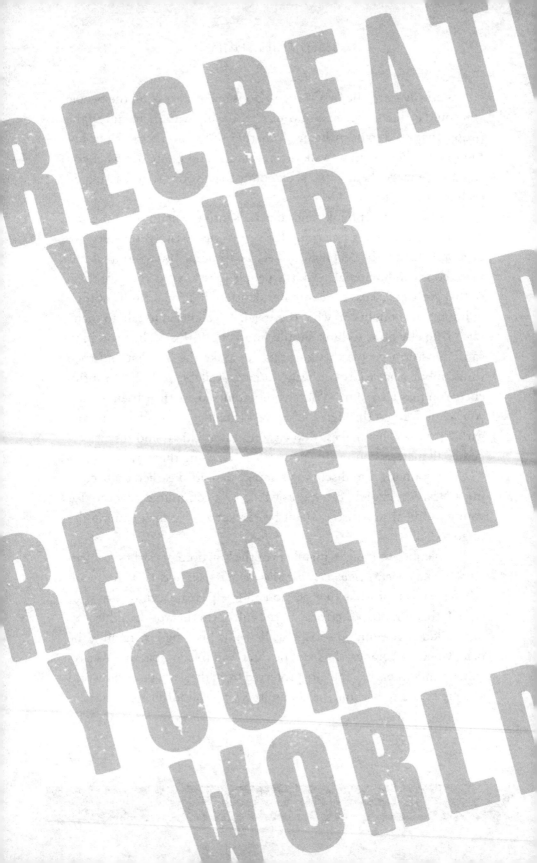

CHAPTER 15

YOUR DREAM
IS YOUR VOICE

You have seen a glimpse of how the world is trying to shape you with their dreams. You see what it is doing to people like Britney and so many of your peers who you have read stories about. You have heard about the Dream Killers and how they demolish your creativity and keep you from becoming a dreamer. You learned about Culture Zombies, and hopefully you have ejected yourself out of the Machine. After seeing the real-life success stories and hearing how young people your age are making a difference and making some noise, it's time for you to let your voice be heard. It's time for you to be a part of the solution.

Lifting your voice to change the world doesn't just mean literally straining your vocal chords (although it might be that too). As you dream a dream for how God wants to use you to change your school, your town, your state, and the world, your dream becomes your voice. As you dream, you send a message to the world about the God you serve and how our world ought to be in light of the fact that *He is God*. As you dream, people will be drawn to your dream in the same way all these other dreamers for the world attract people. As people are attracted to your dream, they will be influenced by your heart.

In a very real way, *your dream is your voice*. If you don't dream, you have no voice. We can't just be talkers—what we are against and things we don't like in our culture. It's time for us to dream dreams that make the gospel attractive and winsome. We could dream a dream of maybe starting an orphanage, starting a band, doing something online that changes the world, or—you fill in the blank. As you start dreaming a dream like that, you start affecting peoples' lives and they are drawn deeper to that dream, and then into the heart of God. It is time to start right now. Not when you are 20, out of college, or 25, but *right now*. Can you say *now*? That is right, when you are 13, 14, 15, 16 or 17. Make a difference dreaming a dream. Scroll down this quick checklist with me.

- Do you have a desire to do something—anything? What might it be?
- Do you have any kind of idea of a talent you might have: technical, computer, sports, music or arts? Is there any way to use that talent to do something?
- Have you thought about venturing on a mission trip during your summer break (you could go by yourself or bring a group with you)? How cool would it be to go to Africa or Asia into a village that has *never heard* the name of Jesus and you get to be the first one to tell them?
- Have you thought about making a specific goal for this year? What are you going to do to make this world a different place? Ask yourself, *What am I going to do to impact people? What dream do I have for this year of my life?*
- Begin dreaming big for your life—*some big, audacious goals.* Most people who did great things for God started by dreaming big while they were still young. Start dreaming big right now. You are never too young to start dreaming. I would encourage you to begin right now, make a commitment, saying, "I refuse to let a year go by without dreaming God's dream for my life and doing something about it." It's a holy determination that says, "I have got to do this or else. I am not going to let my freshman/sophomore/junior/senior year of high school slip by without doing something incredible for God." We know He likes to use regular people like you and me.

Finally I just want to tell you that we are all counting on you to dream a dream for your generation and for your life. This is not a polite little invitation, "Please dream a dream; please be a dreamer . . ." I don't know how to say it any clearer than this—YOU MUST DREAM! If you don't dream, someone else will dream on behalf of your generation.

IF YOU DON'T DREAM, SOMEONE ELSE WILL DREAM ON BEHALF OF YOUR GENERATION. YOUR GENERATION IS COUNTING ON YOU!

They will be the guys who make pornography or write horrible music and terrible television programs. If you don't dream and draw people to the Lord through your dreams, then other people *will* dream. *Somebody* is going to dream a dream and shape your generation. You must dream. We are counting on you. Your generation is counting on you.

There are people on the other side of your dream. If you don't dream, they are not going to get reached. If you don't dream, their life is not going to be affected by the gospel. There you have it. Your opportunity begins right now. I want to encourage you right now as you put this book down to think about the actions you are going to take. Scratch some notes in the back of the book or on some of the stories that you read that have provoked your curiosity. Or jot down some of the ideas inside you that you might want to do. Set the book down right now. Sketch out a rough dream of the things you might want to do. If you could do anything for God, what would you do this next year? Scratch it down right here and then commit it all to the Lord with this simple prayer:

> *Lord Jesus, I thank You that You put me in this world*
> *for a reason. I may be young, but I'm not too young to have*
> *a dream for You. Gideon, David, Mark and Timothy are*
> *all examples of young people who dreamed. They dreamed*
> *for You while they were young and did great things.*
> *Lord, I commit these ideas, dreams and thoughts to You and*
> *ask You to use me NOW to affect my school, community*
> *and my world for the truth of the gospel.*
> *In the name of Jesus, amen.*

Please get online at www.BattleCry.com and let us know what your dream is. Let us know what action you are taking. Join a community of dreamers all over America and around the world who want to take the world back for Jesus—and they're doing something about it while they are young. God bless you. I look forward to seeing you online. I look forward to seeing you on my blog site.

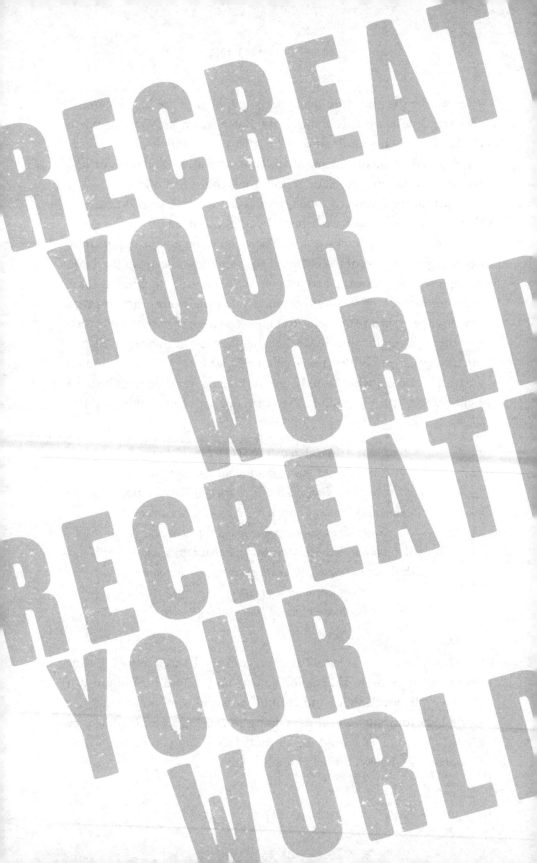

ENDNOTES

Chapter 1: Generation Out of Control

1. Corey Moss, "Madonna Smooches with Britney and Christina; Justin, Coldplay Win Big at VMAs," *MTV.com*, August 28, 2003. http://www.mtv.com/news/articles/1477729/20030828/spears_britney.jhtml?headlines=true (accessed May 2008).
2. Jeff Leeds, "Spears's Awards Fiasco Stirs Speculation About Her Future," *New York Times*, September 13, 2007. http://www.nytimes.com/2007/09/13/arts/music/13brit.html (accessed May 2008).
3. "Winehouse Dominates Grammys with 5 Wins," Associated Press, February 11, 2008. http://www.msnbc.msn.com/id/23100297/ (accessed May 2008).
4. "Annual Estimates of the Population by Sex and Five-Year Age Groups for the United States: April 1, 2000 to July 1, 2007," U.S. Census Bureau. http://www.census.gov/popest/national/asrh/NC-EST2007-sa.html (accessed May 2008).
5. Lauren Ohayon, "I Need It, Mommy!" *That Money Show*, WNET New York. http://www.pbs.org/wnet/moneyshow/cover/111000.html (accessed May 2008).
6. Stefanie Olsen, "Teens and Media: a Full-time Job," *CNET News.com*, December 7, 2006. http://www.news.com/2100-1041_3-6141920.html (accessed May 2008).
7. Douglas Rushkoff, "Merchants of Cool." *Frontline*. http://www.pbs.org/wgbh/pages/frontline/shows/cool/view/ (accessed May 2008).
8. "Viacom Profit Rises on Asset Sale, 'Transformers,'" *Reuters*, November 2, 2007. http://www.cnbc.com/id/21593581/ (accessed May 2008).
9. "12-Year-Old Beats Toddler to Death with Bat, Police Say." Associated Press, January 6, 2008. http://www.cnn.com/2008/CRIME/01/06/infant.killed.ap/ (accessed May 2008).
10. "Teacher Arrested After Offering Good Grades for Oral Sex," Associated Press, December 21, 2007. http://www.foxnews.com/story/0,2933,317611,00.html (accessed May 2008).
11. Jeremy P. Meyer, "Birth Leave Sought for Girls," *The Denver Post*, January 7, 2008. http://www.denverpost.com/news/ci_7899096 (accessed May 2008).
12. "Colorado Teens Accused of Killing 7-year-old Girl with 'Mortal Kombat' Game Moves," Associated Press, December 20, 2007. http://www.foxnews.com/story/0,2933,317544,00.html (accessed May 2008).
13. "Teen Accused of Trying to Rape a 62-year-old Woman," *ABC2News*, January 10, 2008. http://www.topix.com/editor/profile/abc2news (accessed May 2008).
14. "6th-grade Teacher Gets 10 Years in Prison for Sex with 13-year-old Boy," Associated Press, March 17, 2007. http://www.foxnews.com/story/0,2933,259370,00.html (accessed May 2008).
15. "Mom: Michigan Teen Shooter Stopped Taking Medication Before Killing," Associated Press, March 9, 2007. http://www.foxnews.com/story/0,2933,258023,00.html (accessed May 2008).
16. "Nevada Suspect Arraigned in Case of Videotaped Rape of Girl, 3," *Fox News*, October 17, 2007. http://www.foxnews.com/story/0,2933,302529,00.html (accessed May 2008).
17. "U.S. Prosecutor Accused of Seeking Sex with Girl, 5," *Fox News*, September 18, 2007. http://www.foxnews.com/story/0,2933,297152,00.html (accessed May 2008).
18. "Cops: Texas Girl, 6, Found Hanging in Garage Was Sexually Abused," *Fox News*, September 12, 2007. http://www.foxnews.com/story/0,2933,296585,00.html (accessed May 2008).
19. "Michigan Mom Gets 12 to 22 Years for Sex 'Contract' on Underage Daughter," Associated Press, June 19, 2007. http://www.foxnews.com/story/0,2933,284255,00.html (accessed May 2008).
20. "Man Gets 20 Years for Bizarre Internet Love Triangle Murder," Associated Press, November 27, 2007. http://www.foxnews.com/story/0,2933,313343,00.html (accessed May 2008).
21. "Four College Students Shot Execution-style in Newark, N.J." Associated Press, August 6, 2007. http://www.foxnews.com/story/0,2933,292200,00.html (accessed May 2008).
22. "Young Mother Charged After Her 10-month-old Boy Recorded Sipping Gin and Juice," Associated Press, June 23, 2007. http://www.foxnews.com/story/0,2933,286193,00.html (accessed May 2008).

Chapter 3: The Insidious Grip of Culture

1. "Insidious," *Dictionary.com Unabridged (v 1.1)*. Random House, Inc. http://dictionary.refer ence.com/browse/insidious (accessed July 2008).
2. "Lions," Wikipedia, The Free Encyclopedia. http://en.wikipedia.org/wiki/Lion
3. Judith Kohler, "Colorado Church Gunman Had Been Kicked Out," *Brietbart.com*, December 10, 2007. http://www.breitbart.com/article.php?id=D8TEUPFG0&show_article=1 (accessed May 2008); "Church Gunman Left Online Rant Between Shootings," *Denver News*, December 11, 2007. http://www.thedenverchannel.com/news/14822541/detail.html (accessed May 2008).
4. Lynn Bartels and Carla Crowder, "Fatal Friendship," *Rocky Mountain News*, August 22, 1999. http://denver.rockymountainnews.com/shooting/0822fata1.shtml (accessed May 2008).
5. "Jamie Lynn Spears Biography (1991-)," Biography.com. http://www.biography.com/search/article.do?id=262390&page=print (accessed May 2008).
6. Ben Thompson, "Tell Us Your Story," *Honor Academy Intern*, January 2008.

Chapter 9: Dreamers Always Win (the Culture War)

1. "The Big Five of Commercial Media," World-Information.org. http://world-information.org/wio/infostructure/100437611795/100438659010 (accessed May 2008).
2. Laurie Goodstein, "Evangelicals Fear the Loss of Their Teenagers," *New York Times*, October 6, 2006. http://www.nytimes.com/2006/10/06/us/06evangelical.html?_r=1&sq=Ron%20Luce&st=nyt&adxnnl=1&oref=slogin&scp=4&adxnnlx=1209582050-VudW4yeTjRmHr3NjBDsqcQ (accessed July 2008).

Chapter 10: Paralyzed by the Ordinary

1. "More on the Britney-Madonna Kiss!" Associated Press, September 5, 2003. http://www.cbs news.com/stories/2003/09/05/entertainment/main571865.shtml (accessed May 2008).

Chapter 12: Real-Life Success Stories

1. "Youth Group Protests Store's 'Pornaments,'" *News4Jax.com*, December 6, 2006. http://www.news4jax.com/news/10479455/detail.html (accessed May 2008).
2. "Top Ten Facts About Modern Slavery," Free the Slaves, 2007. http://www.freetheslaves.net/NETCOMMUNITY/Page.aspx?pid=375&srcid=424 (accessed May 2008).
3. Jana Riess, "Abolitionist Teen Speaks Out Against Modern-day Slavery," *Religion BookLine*, February 21, 2007. http://www.publishersweekly.com/article/CA6418085.html (accessed May 2008); Interviews with Zach can be found at www.myspace.com/lc2lc (accessed May 2008).
4. "Mayor Michael Sessions," City of Hillsdale. http://www.ci.hillsdale.mi.us/sessions.htm (accessed May 2008).
5. Jordan Kintner "Tell Us Your Story," *Honor Academy Intern*, August 2007-2008.
6. Brianna Keleher, "Tell Us Your Story," *Honor Academy Intern*, January 2008.

Chapter 13: Are We Not Dreamers?

1. "Number of Sexual Scenes on TV Nearly Double Since 1998," The Henry J. Kaiser Family Foundation, November 9, 2005. http://www.kff.org/entmedia/entmedia110905nr.cfm (accessed July 2008).
2. Casey Williams, "MTV Smut Peddlers: Targeting Kids with Sex, Drugs, and Alcohol," Parents Television Council, March 2004. http://www.parentstv.org/PTC/publications/reports/mtv2005/main.asp (accessed May 2008).
3. Berry, Sandra H., Rebecca L. Collins, Marc N. Elliot, et al, "Watching Sex on Television Predicts Adolescents Initiation of Sexual Behavior," *Pediatrics* 114, no. 3 (2004): e280-e289. http://pediatrics.aappublications.org/cgi/content/full/114/3/e280 (accessed May 2008).
4. Roger Friedman, "No Buyers for Dakota Fanning Rape Movie," *Fox News*, January 25, 2007. http://www.foxnews.com/story/0,2933,246698,00.html (accessed May 2008).
5. Dr. Macenstein, "Bill Gates Spies on His Kids, Limits Internet Access," Macenstein, February 21, 2007. http://macenstein.com/default/archives/538 (accessed May 2008).
6. "Cruise and Spielberg Limit Their Kids' TV Viewing," *Hellomagazine.com*, September 27, 2002. http://www.hellomagazine.com/film/2002/09/27/cruisespielberg (accessed May 2008).

Teen Mania's Mission Statement:

To provoke a young generation to passionately pursue Jesus Christ and to take His life-giving message to the ends of the earth!

Acquire the Fire

*Since 1991, Acquire the Fire has been providing young people with a weekend-long event packed with drama, pyrotechnics, powerful worship, uplifting messages, and music from some of the best bands on the Christian music scene. Hundreds of thousands of teens from across North America have come away with lifelong friendships, a renewed hope for their future, and a peace that can only come from Christ! **Join the movement that is sweeping North America!** More than 2 million teens have been exposed and challenged to a life-long pursuit of Jesus Christ. Go to www.acquirethefire.com to find out when we are coming to a city near you.*

Center for Creative Media

The Center for Creative Media is dedicated to training young innovators, filmmakers, designers and creative talent to influence their culture with the message of the gospel by providing hands-on opportunities to receive training from industry experts, gain experience with Hollywood, and influence modern culture. The Center for Creative Media is a full-fledged production company that creates and produces television broadcasts, live events, DVDs, websites, curriculum, music videos and much more. This exciting two-year program is open to all high-school graduates. For more information, visit www.centerforcreativemedia.com

Global Expeditions

In a youth culture that idolizes personal gain and self gratification, Teen Mania's Global Expeditions missions trips are committed to providing life-changing short-term mission trip endeavors for teens who are serious about changing their world. Each participant receives in-depth training to minister alongside churches and missionaries through drama, building projects, personal evangelism and church planting. More than 1.2 millions decisions for Christ have been made in 80 different countries as a result of these trips. Check out www.globalexpeditions.org for needs all over the world that you can help to meet.

Honor Academy

Today, there are more than 4,000 Honor Academy Alumni impacting their generation for Christ. These strong men and women complete a year-long intensive leadership training internship that revolutionizes their lives through intensive spiritual training and leadership opportunities that enable them to gain a foundational biblical worldview and practical hands-on ministry experience. Many receive further specialized training in a second- and third-year track. Regional braches are opening all over the nation. Additional individual training includes specialized tracks for writing (taught by Shannon Ethridge), worship (supervised by Paul Baloche), missions in partnership (with Bethany College in Minnesota) and more. Interns are also able to earn college credits for some of the classes taught during the year. For information on this life-changing opportunity, go to www.honoracademy.org.

To Contact Us:

1-800-299-3473
info@teenmania.org
Teen Mania Ministries
PO Box 2000
Garden Valley, TX 75771

www.teenmania.org